THE UNHAPPY DOG:

Overcoming Separation Anxiety, Aggression, Depression and Other Behavioural Upsets

BY THE SAME AUTHOR:

Simply Raw: A Guide for Raw Feeding your Dog
Train Your Dog to Read: The Complete Guide to Clicker Training

Published internationally by Present Perfect Press, Melton Mowbray, United Kingdom.

For Frank

CONTENTS

FOREWORD

Throughout this book, I refer to several 'example' dogs who are all based on ones I have encountered during my experience as a behaviourist. The first of these I'd like to mention right now, because he was one of the first dogs I worked with, and because what I observed with him proved to be a useful frame of reference for later experiences.

His name was Percy, an elderly Clumber spaniel. He belonged to one of my neighbours, an equally elderly lady who knew that I had an interest in, and was studying, canine behaviour. This neighbour had asked for my advice regarding Percy's unappetising behaviour on his daily walk in the park; keen to build up my practical experience, I offered to accompany her and see what Percy got up to.

During the walk, Percy's owner did several things which perhaps seem natural and understandable in the circumstances, but which turn out to be quite unhelpful. I'll briefly recreate the walk; see if you can spot her 'mistakes'.

Our walk through the park began at a slow trudge with Percy being rather unwillingly tugged along at the end of his lead. My neighbour was explaining that Percy had become a bit 'grumpy' on his walks, which she had recently taken charge of in place of her husband, whose knees were getting too troublesome. As we continued, she told me that Percy had started to become quite obstinate, often stopping in his tracks, sitting down, and refusing to move forward. So far, he was refusing to reproduce this behaviour, and plodded along stoically behind us. Nevertheless, my neighbour stopped several times to indicate the sorts of things that might trigger his immobility: a brightly coloured sign, a man pushing a buggy, a cyclist, ducks quacking on the pond.

She paused again to indicate a particularly troubling obstacle: at a point beside the pond a family had gathered to feed the ducks, and a little terrier was yapping excitedly around them. Sure enough, we had reached the climactic moment of the walk. Percy, upon noticing the spectacle, froze immediately. A slight growl emerged from his throat.

'Best just ignore him,' insisted my neighbour, tugging again on Percy's lead. Eyes rooted on the noisy terrier, he wasn't going to budge.

I blame myself at least a bit for what happened next, because I asked my neighbour what she would normally do in this sort of situation. She immediately demonstrated by grabbing Percy's collar and attempting to haul him forward. Her intention was to exert firm control over her dog, but the result was a dramatic flare in Percy's anxiety, which he vented by snapping sharply at his owner. She sprang back from him, embarrassed, hiding the red mark on her hand. 'Come on then, this way,' she said brusquely, and steered Percy back in the direction from which we had come.

The short remainder of the walk took on a sombre mood as she repeatedly assured me that Percy had never been quite that naughty before, always keeping the wounded hand out of sight behind her back.

Percy was lucky to have such an owner as my elderly neighbour, who was so conscientious about his wellbeing. But despite her best efforts, there were several things that should have been avoided or done differently on this walk. Let's look through them:

- o The tugging is quite an obvious detraction. It caused physical discomfort, which would have exacerbated Percy's anxiety, and may even have become a trigger if he learned to associate the tug with his anxious feelings.

- o The stopping. The owner stopped each time a possible trigger for Percy's anxiety was nearby, which would have alerted Percy to something being amiss and may have contributed to the triggering of his anxiety.

- o 'Best just ignore him.' In a sense, the owner was quite right here. Pretending to ignore the dog when he shows signs of anxiety is preferable to consoling him, which would only affirm his need to be anxious. But the owner's subsequent action contradicted her own advice to ignore him.

- o Grabbing Percy's collar and trying to physically move him closer to the source of consternation is, of course, likely to inflame his anxiety.

- o Finally, turning Percy away from the trigger and walking in the opposite direction sends him the message that behaving in this way will get him what he wants – to be away from the source of his anxiety. He will therefore learn to repeat the behaviour next time he is in a similar situation.

You'll no doubt have spotted that, as the supposed expert, I was not free from blame either. The experience taught me much about my own conduct as a behaviourist, which is one of the reasons I think back to it so frequently.

If my neighbour were to pick up this book, what part of it should she turn to for help? The book is divided into several sections, each dealing with a specific behavioural upset. But Percy didn't just have one clear issue he needs help with; instead, several were interlinked. His fear-induced anxiety resulted in aggression toward his owner, but it also seems as if his relationship with the owner was not as secure as it could be. He was used to being taken for walks by the husband, and didn't quite trust the leadership of the wife. So leadership anxiety played a role, too. It's also possible that his old age was having an effect, perhaps making elements of a once-familiar environment seem alien and threatening – this means he needed help with environmental anxiety.

The next chapter is designed to help 'diagnose' your dog's unhappiness and to give an idea of what sort of anxiety or upset might be causing problems. But in most cases, as with Percy, there will be more than one issue at play. I hope that reading through the other chapters, as well as the one which the diagnostic quiz indicates as the primary concern, will give a good understanding about how best to help your dog.

A final note before continuing: this book is designed to give understanding about various upsets that might be making a dog unhappy, and to give some practical suggestions toward alleviating those upsets. It should not, however, replace the advice of a professional behaviourist delivered on a one-to-one, personal basis. Such advice can be tailored to your dog's particular needs and personality, and is the best way to get help.

.

Help!

In the next chapter, we'll look at a range of different anxieties and upsets which could be troubling your dog; but first, let's hear from some owners who need urgent diagnosis and advice for some of the more urgent or distressing behavioural issues.

1.

I have recently adopted a rescue dog who is frightened of everything. She is always crying, shies away from us when we try to get near her, and can't seem to sleep or even be calm for any significant period of time. She's been with us for nearly a week and we thought she would be starting to feel at least a bit settled by now, but it seems to be getting worse. Should we take her back to the rescue shelter?

In such cases, anxiety isn't triggered by any single or specific stimulus; instead, the behaviour is born from the dog's general state of nervousness and fear. This dog needs help with her FEAR-INDUCED ANXIETY (p56) first of all.

If no progress can be made there, then it is probably because the new environment, or elements of it, are exacerbating her nervousness. So the owner will need to address the dog's ENVIRONMENTAL ANXIETY (p205).

As soon as the fear-induced anxiety is diminished to the extent that the owner can begin to engage with the dog without triggering further anxiety, the owner should attune the dog to the clicker. This is an effective, efficient way to give the dog a much-needed sense of security, and will help begin to develop the dog-owner relationship. Then, while continuing to work on overcoming the fear-induced anxiety, the owner should also follow the advice in LEADERSHIP ANXIETY (p129) to further strengthen the relationship. When she starts to feel secure under the new owner's leadership, the dog will become much more settled and self-assured.

2.

My dog barks all the time whenever he's let outdoors and the neighbours are getting ready to lynch him

If this is a change in behaviour, there is a possibility it could indicate that the dog is feeling discomfort and should be checked over by a vet. Usually, this sort of barking is caused by some form of anxiety. In the more explicit sense, it could be that something happened to the dog in the garden to cause him distress (stung by a wasp; spooked by a helicopter) and he is now acting defensively. More commonly, habitual barking like this is caused by a mix of leadership anxiety and territorial aggression.

In that case, it won't look like anxiety - it will look as if he's having a delightful time. But he has taken on the 'leader's' role of protecting the territory of the garden - from absolutely anything that meets his (not very picky) criteria for being a threat or intruder.

It speaks of a dog who doesn't have a clear appreciation of the owner's role as leader, so LEADERSHIP ANXIETY would give help.

In the more immediate term, the owner should stop 'letting' the dog outside, and start 'taking' him outside - in a controlled, positive way which rewards his calm obedience to heeling on the lead with generous praise and treats. Being taken outside under the owner's control and leadership will help make the dog feel much more secure, much happier, and less anxious - so he won't feel the need to bark. But if/when his calmness does break, we use negative punishment (and the only form of punishment I ever advocate using) by taking him back indoors. This is 'negative punishment' because it deprives the dog of something he valued - his time outside - and sends the message that the behaviour he exhibited (rowdy barking) will result in his desired object being taken from him.

Consistent and persistent work on improving the dog-owner relationship, as explored in the leadership-anxiety section, will see more long-term and more stable improvements in the dog's general behaviour.

3.

My dog is aggressive! He's nipped visitors we've had in our house, and he's even tried to nip people who've approached us during walks.

Without knowing more about the dog, it is difficult to know whether this aggressive behaviour is provoked by FEAR-INDUCED ANXIETY, ASSOCIATIVE-MEMORY ANXIETY (p185) or TRIGGERED ANXIETY (p215). However, the way we alleviate all those anxieties involves similar conditioning methods which aim to rewire the associations the dog identifies in the anxiety trigger, so the owner should look through those sections and decide which approach is most appropriate for her dog's particular issues.

The great difficulty here lies in ensuring the safety of others while the owner and dog work to alleviate the anxiety. If the dog does not yet wear a muzzle, then the owner should forget the stigma and buy one for her dog. WEARING A MUZZLE (p239) will show how to introduce the dog to it in a positive, comfortable way. Needless to say, the owner has made the necessary adjustments to the dog's lifestyle - keeping him secure when visitors arrive; keeping him under firm control when walking - that ensure the safety of others.

Again, working on the dog's leadership anxiety will, with persistence, bring great benefit to the dog's general sense of security and will make him become a less anxious and nippy dog.

DIAGNOSING DOG UNHAPPINESS

We first need to understand the source of the dog's upsets in order to effectively overcome them.

UNHAPPINESS OR ILLNESS?

A crucial step, which you have probably already taken, is to be absolutely sure that your dog's unhappiness is not symptomatic of an underlying illness.

Illnesses and physical pain can cause dogs to exhibit signs of anxiety. If he is suffering, you may well be noticing changes in his behaviour such as him becoming nervous of people (even you) approaching him, pacing, trembling, hiding, becoming lethargic, and having his tail tucked between his legs. His increased sense of vulnerability may cause him to lash out when he is approached.

If you see this sort of behavioural change, and if it seems quite sudden, it could be a sign of illness or injury. Loss of appetite, diarrhoea, vomiting and limping are among the signs which may accompany this behavioural change if it is due to illness.

Speak to a vet as soon as possible if you have any suspicion that your dog's anxious behaviour may be due to illness or injury.

WHAT SORT OF UPSET?

Once we are sure the dog's behaviour is not related to an underlying illness, we need to investigate the precise nature of his anxiety or fear.

As a first diagnostic step, the following 'quiz' may help you determine what sort of anxiety or fear is troubling your dog.

STEP 1: My dog only shows anxiety or fear in certain situations.

A. YES: (he only gets upset in certain situations) go to STEP 5.
B. NO: (he is generally anxious/fearful/upset most of the time) go to STEP 2.

STEP 2: My dog's anxiety manifests in aggressive behaviour towards myself or other people.

A. YES: (he tends to snap at me, other people, and/or other dogs) go to RESULTS: AGGRESSION.
B. YES: (he only snaps at me) go to RESULTS: LEADERSHIP ANXIETY.
C. NO: (he doesn't show aggression, he is just generally nervous, quiet and withdrawn) go to STEP 3.

STEP 3: My dog's unhappiness has coincided with a recent change of environment such as a house move.

A. YES: go to RESULTS: ENVIRONMENTAL ANXIETY.
B. NO: go to STEP 4.

STEP 4: Despite being quiet, withdrawn, etc., my dog is generally obedient and well behaved.

A. YES: go to RESULTS: DEPRESSION.
B. NO: go to RESULTS: LEADERSHIP ANXIETY.

STEP 5: There is a clear stimulus which provokes my dog's unhappiness.

A. YES: loud noises. Go to RESULTS: NOISE ANXIETY.
B. YES: travel in the car. Go to RESULTS: TRAVEL ANXIETY.
C. YES: being touched. Go to RESULTS: TOUCH ANXIETY.
D. YES: certain types of people (men, a person carrying a stick, etc.). Go to RESULTS: ASSOCIATIVE-MEMORY ANXIETY.
E. YES: another specific stimulus (vacuum cleaner, going to the vets, etc.). Go to RESULTS: ASSOCIATIVE-MEMORY ANXIETY.
F. YES: but not always the same stimulus. Go to RESULTS: TRIGGERED ANXIETY.
G. NO: go to STEP 6.

STEP 6: My dog's unhappiness manifests in aggressive behaviour toward other people or animals.

A. YES: go to RESULTS: AGGRESSION.
B. NO: go to STEP 7.

STEP 7: My dog is only unhappy when I am away from him.

    A.   YES: go to RESULTS: SEPARATION ANXIETY.
    B.   NO: go to RESULTS: ENVIRONMENTAL ANXIETY.

RESULTS

If the diagnosis quiz above hasn't lead you to a clearer definition of your dog's unhappiness, then reading through the following sections might help you link it to a specific source.

Aggression

You probably don't need the help of a quiz to diagnose this. Any form of threatening behaviour from your dog counts as aggression. This can range from lip twitching, growling, snarling, and barking (all of which are likely accompanied by direct eye contact) all the way up to attacking and biting.

There are many different reasons why a dog might show aggression. It may be induced by fear – if he feels vulnerable or threatened, he will meet this with aggression. Some dogs are genetically disposed to be aggressive, and this doesn't necessarily depend on the breed. Any dog can have aggressive tendencies passed down from his ancestry, whether bred through selection or by coincidence.

Aggression can be shown from dogs who feel the need to protect someone or something. An aggressive dog may be trying to protect his territory (your house or garden) or his 'pack' (you and your family) from a perceived threat.

It is quite natural for dogs to show aggression in a social context. When living in a group, young dogs will establish a natural identification of who is the parental or leadership figure of their pack. If they feel that the parent/leader is missing or not capable of leading, they may seek to fulfil the position themselves. The human owner can become embroiled in this – if your dog doesn't have a clear respect for your position as parent/leader, it may cause him to exhibit aggressive tendencies toward you (see LEADERSHIP ANXIETY, p129).

Some dogs can be very protective over their food, toys, bed, etc. They can become aggressive when they feel another dog or human is threatening to remove any of these things from them. This is known as 'resource guarding'.

Unfortunately, it is easy for these forms of aggression to have a snowballing effect in dogs. If they learn that their aggressive behaviour gets them what they want, they will feel encouraged to repeat it. For example, if your dog snaps at you when you try to take a favourite toy away from him and you (quite understandably) withdraw, he is getting what he wants (which is for you to leave him alone with his toy). He learns that this aggressive behaviour earns the desired outcome, and will repeat it.

Similarly, because of their associative memory, dogs quite quickly learn to become aggressive toward anything which they recognise as having caused them distress in the past. So, if a child was a bit too playful with him when he was a puppy, and caused him distress, he will learn to associate children with his distress. The result is that he becomes defensive and possibly aggressive toward other children.

The AGGRESSION section (p27) will give guidance on how to help a dog who is exhibiting any of these types of aggression.

However, you should also be watchful for aggression which is provoked by illness or injury. A dog who is feeling ill or in pain will likely become more self-protective in his vulnerable state. Check that this isn't the cause of your dog's aggression, and contact your vet if you suspect he is unwell.

Associative-memory anxiety

Dogs have a very different type of memory to humans — and the difference can help explain some of their unhappy behaviour.

Unlike humans, dogs are very bad at recalling specific information from their memory. If you think back to what you were doing five hours ago, you will most likely be able to recall in vivid detail where you were, what you were doing, how you felt, etc. Dogs can't do that. They have very poor short-term memory. Even something that happened as recently as two minutes ago will be lost to the oblivion of your dog's forgetfulness. It is an eerie thought, but when you return home from work and greet your dog, he won't remember when you said goodbye in the morning.

Dogs' long-term memory works purely through association. Your dog remembers you by learning to associate your smell, appearance and manner with the thing they identify as being their 'master', parent or leader. He associates you with the feeling of comfort he experiences when you show him affection. He gets excited whenever you fetch his lead from the cupboard because he has learned to associate that action with going out for a walk. Many dogs get unhappy when they leap out of the car and find themselves at the vets because they have learned to associate that place, along with all its particular smells and noises, with the sensation of discomfort when getting jabbed by a needle.

This association-driven memory is a powerful force. Associations become very strong once established. This is great in some regards — it allows us to build strong relationships with our dogs — but it also means less positive associations are hard to remove.

Associative-memory anxiety is therefore quite a common issue in dogs who have been rescued from unpleasant homes or situations where they have experienced neglect and abuse. These poor things have learned to associate humans with pain; it requires great patience and compassion on our part to mitigate this.

If your dog is frightened of men (or shows aggression toward them), or people carrying sticks, or people with beards, or people wearing a certain style of hat, it is likely because his memory associates these symbols with an unpleasant experience. The section ASSOCIATIVE-MEMORY ANXIETY (p185) gives guidance on how to weaken these associations and help the unhappiness they induce in your dog.

Depression

Whilst 'unhappiness' in dogs is often due to some sort of fear or anxiety, it may also be very literal. Dogs can experience depression just like people do.

Boredom, a lack of fulfilment, a change in routine or circumstances, a lack of companionship and a lack of stimulation are among the possible stimulants of depression.

A depressed dog will appear unusually quiet and withdrawn. He may be reluctant to go outside into the garden or to go for his walk. His spark for life might seem to have been extinguished. Destructive behaviour, such as chewing your furniture, could also be a marker of depression. It may be that your dog is naturally a bit quiet and there's actually nothing wrong, but if he was previously a live wire then the change in behaviour probably means he has started to feel a bit depressed. The DEPRESSION section (p151) will give ideas about how to help cheer him up.

Leadership anxiety

Dogs are, by law of nature, pack animals. They define themselves around a firmly ingrained sense of hierarchy, and to feel comfortable they need to have a clear identification of who leads their pack.

Even if the 'pack' consists of just you and your dog, your relationship is still underlined by all the socio-political orchestrations that determine whether it's you or your dog who is the parent/leader figure. Just as with the teacher who can't establish a dominant position in the class, if there is no clear leader then everything falls apart and no one is happy.

Some ambitious dogs will want to climb the hierarchy and establish themselves as parent/leader over you. Look for signs that your dog is not respecting your parental position – he might be disobedient, or snap at you when you exhibit a leader-like authority.

Other than ambition, it may be that he feels you are not doing a satisfactory job as leader and therefore decides he has no option but to assume the position himself. Sloppy leadership on the owner's part puts this uncomfortable burden on the dog, which may make him stressed and unhappy.

Whether it's his natural ambition to climb the hierarchy or an identity crisis due to the owner's poor leadership, neither scenario is the dog's fault. He just needs the owner to step up and more clearly fulfil the parent/leader role. He won't mind being subordinate to the owner at all – in fact a lot of dogs, like people, are uncomfortable with the responsibility of leadership – he just needs clear understanding of who is boss so he feels secure with his own position.

Of course, there are right ways and wrong ways for the owner to assert leadership, and a wrong way would be using force and fear to dominate the dog. A fearful dog is only going to have his anxieties exacerbated. See the section 'LEADERSHIP ANXIETY' (p129) for ideas about how to forge a parent/leader position in a healthy way.

Separation anxiety

Separation anxiety is a very common woe of the modern dog, and one that causes many owners a huge amount of guilt. It is not difficult to diagnose.

Dogs who become hyperactive before you leave for work and when you return, dogs who go on destructive rampages when you are out of the house, dogs who elicit complaints from the neighbours because they've been howling and barking themselves hoarse while you're away, dogs who scratch and chew at the bottom of your door, and dogs who wee and poo in the house when left alone can all join the not-particularly-exclusive club of separation-anxiety sufferers.

Because dogs are inherently pack animals, they naturally feel discomfort when separated from their pack. Some breeds (including German Shepherds, Vizslas and Border Collies, among others) seem more prone to suffer from it than others, but none are entirely immune. The problem is compounded by dogs' very poor short-term memory. They have no appreciation of the amount of time you have been away, nor can they get a good sense of how long it will be before you get back home. Whereas a human has the security of knowing that his parent/partner will be home by five o'clock, this sort of prediction is inaccessible to your dog which makes periods of absence all the more intolerable.

Helping a dog who suffers from being left alone largely revolves in helping them become more confident and comfortable in your absence. See the section entitled 'SEPARATION ANXIETY' (p99) for guidance on how to achieve this.

Environmental anxiety

Environmental anxiety is a fairly broad category of dog unhappiness, but largely falls into two types.

Firstly, your dog may be unhappy with the environment you provide for him at home. His unhappiness may manifest in tendencies to try and escape by burrowing at the door or under the fence in your garden; he may find it hard to settle for rest and might keep you awake with lots of noise at night; he might seem nervous while at home and will be reticent when you show him affection; he might exhibit destructive tendencies such as damaging furniture; he might exhibit strong nervous behaviour such as eating his own poo.

Secondly, 'environmental anxiety' can also refer to any distress your dog experiences when he is subjected to an environment or context he is not comfortable with. You might find your dog gets anxious when walking through town, or when you meet a group of unknown people, or any other situation he is not used to. This sort of anxiety is particularly common for dogs who went through sheltered puppyhoods where they weren't given early exposure to a wide range of experiences.

The section 'ENVIRONMENTAL ANXIETY' (p205) will help you tackle it in both its forms.

Travel anxiety

My Newfoundland, Frank, liked to stick his head out of the car window and feel the breeze in his hair and against his flappy jowls – but not many dogs take car journeys so comfortably.

Not only is the experience of a car journey one which is naturally alien and disorientating for dogs, but it's also one which puts their associative memories to powerful work in aligning them against it. If your dog resists getting into the car and shows distress when travelling, it is likely because he associates the experience with the nausea he felt when travelling as a puppy – even if he no longer feels sick as an adult. Or, he associates getting in the car with arriving somewhere unpleasant, like the vets.

See 'TRAVEL ANXIETY' (p203) for help with making him a happy passenger.

Noise anxiety

Sometimes, there's no obscurely hidden cause for your dog's anxiety – it's simply triggered as an instinctive, but rational, response to a frightening stimulus. A lot of dogs are fearful of loud noises or particular noises not because there's some deep-rooted association between the noise and an unpleasant experience, but because the noise is naturally frightening for them.

There are several steps we can take to make our dogs more comfortable when they have no option but to be subjected to these unpleasant noises ('bonfire night' being a prime example). Refer to the 'NOISE ANXIETY' section (p199) for details.

Touch anxiety

There are various reasons why a dog might shy away from being touched. A lot of dogs do not like to be touched on their sensitive paws, and dogs who have been unfortunate to suffer abuse in a previous home may not wish to be touched on any part of their body. This can cause problems when handling the dog is necessary, and also prevents the dog's new, caring owner from being able to show affection. The section 'GROOMING/TOUCH ANXIETY' (p218) will offer help for overcoming this anxiety.

Triggered anxiety

A triggered anxiety is one which is induced as the result of a particular stimulus where there is no underlying association and the fear response seems irrational (unlike noise anxiety).

Triggered anxieties can come in an array of forms. Some dogs are frightened of lawnmowers; others don't like bin liners. Most dogs will have some sort of trigger that gives them the spooks, and it may not be much of a problem if it's not something the dog encounters very often. Sometimes, however, the trigger can be something which can be quite inhibitive to a good quality of life – a dog might be frightened of his food or water bowl, for example, or the trigger might make frequent and unavoidable occurrences in his daily life. The section 'TRIGGERED ANXIETY' (p215) will show you how to help him overcome his nerves.

GENERAL APPROACHES TO HAPPINESS

No matter what the specific root cause of the dog's unhappiness, there are important attitudes we need to adopt in order to help him cheer up.

Positivity

Stressing this is vital, though surely superfluous for the compassionate sort of owners who would go to the trouble of buying a book in order to help their dogs become happier.

Punishing a dog for any sort of anxiety-driven behaviour will not help. Even if said behaviour comes in the form of aggression. The dog behaves this way because he is anxious, fearful, stressed. To serve him punishment as a results only serves to increase his anxiety. It will make him more likely to lash out in a similar future scenario, because he will associate it with the punitive response he received last time and will be even more defensive.

Carefully managed training will reduce the amount of situations where your dog will do anything that some owners might feel merits punishment, but mistakes will inevitably happen on both our part and our dogs'. We must always aim to focus on the positive, rewarding for good behaviour rather than punishing the mistakes.

You are your dog's mirror

In stressful situations, owners can make things worse for their dogs by letting themselves get stressed. Dogs are remarkably sharp at picking up on their owners' feelings. Imagine you are walking with your dog and you see some other walkers with their own dogs approaching. You worry that your dog may start growling at them, so you naturally pull him closer with the lead. Something as simple and seemingly unnoticeable as the increased tension on the lead may alert your dog to your own anxieties, and cause him to become more defensive.

It's a situation novice horse riders, for example, will be very familiar with. When they approach a tractor in a field, or a car comes toward them on the road, they know their horse is going to feel nervous; anticipating the horse's nervousness causes the rider to feel nervous, but the horse picks up on this (through a tighter grip in the rider's feet or more tension on the reins) and becomes even more nervous. It escalates into a calamitous heap of shared nervousness.

When you are working with your dog to help his anxieties, it is therefore very important that you model the calm, controlled attitude you want to see reflected in him. Show him through your own attitude that everything is okay, there is nothing to worry about, and he is more likely to feel the same calm confidence himself.

This means monitoring quite closely everything about your own attitude. No matter what sort of anxiety you are working with – whether it's aggression or a dislike of car journeys – keep your voice and movements consistently calm. Feel relaxed. Exude confidence. Help your dog feel that you are in charge of the situation, so he understands that if you're calm he can be too.

Training your relationship

The happy dog knows that training doesn't begin and end with teaching him to wee outside rather than on the rug. An owner/dog relationship which is constituted by some regular training is hugely powerful in building the dog's confidence and overall happiness.

A trained dog has a better understanding of his owner. He knows what his owner is asking of him, and gets the immense satisfaction of doing something he knows has pleased his master – along with the joy of a tasty reward. It helps him to feel confident; it gives him more fulfilment by providing a function for him to perform, and it also gives clearer definition to the owner's position as parent/leader which helps establish his confidence in the owner.

Doing some regular practice of simple exercises like 'sit', 'down', and 'stay' can be really helpful in this way. But you might find you want to take it a bit further, in which case you could do some clicker training or join an obedience class. The latter option has the immense benefit of introducing your dog to a social environment and building his confidence around other dogs and people. Your instructors will be very supportive (provided they're half decent) with your dog's particular anxieties, and will be full of advice and strategies to help.

Keep it rewarding

In line with the attitude of positivity we need to adopt, we must make sure our dog is being readily rewarded for good behaviour. Keep a generous supply of tasty treats at hand so you can reward him next time he doesn't let his anxieties get the better of him. It'll make him happier, and encourage him to repeat the same behaviour in the future.

Of course, rewards don't always have to be treats. His well-earned reward could be in the form of a big affectionate fuss from his master, or a game with his favourite toy. So long as the reward is something he really enjoys, he'll be happy.

Exercise those endorphins

One thing every unhappy dog needs is a big refreshing blast of joy-fuelling endorphins. Whether he's anxious, frightened or depressed, good invigorating exercise on a regular basis is vital for his overall health and happiness.

Really enjoyable food can also help his mood. You might consider trying him on some raw-meaty bones such as lamb necks, ribs, or bone-in chicken. Eating these sorts of foods, which a dog's teeth are naturally designed to devour, can be a great way to release endorphins and give him a delightful blast of enjoyment.

In the following sections, we'll examine specific sources of unhappiness along with some practical methods for alleviating them. .

AGGRESSION

Aggressive behaviour in dogs is best handled by direct consultation with a behavioural specialist. The information and guidance below is not intended as a replacement for help offered from a professional on a one-to-one basis.

Calm compassion is our mantra here. If a dog exhibits signs of aggression, it doesn't mean he's 'aggressive'. What it really means, for the vast majority of 'aggressive' dogs, is that he's frightened. His aggressive signs are his natural way of responding to a perceived threat of some variety. If we start to think of 'aggressive' dogs as really being 'frightened' dogs, we can begin to see why calm compassion is such a vital attitude for us to adopt when helping them.

Having said that, we mustn't be so calm in our approach that we become blasé about the potential danger our frightened dogs pose, when their anxieties manifest in aggressive forms of behaviour, to other people and dogs in real-world situations. So another mantra we need to adopt is control. We help our dogs in carefully controlled situations, and always ensure we are never putting ourselves, our dogs, or others in jeopardy.

Understanding is the first step in helping, so let's examine the different types of aggressive behaviour to get a better grasp of the specific unhappiness our dogs are suffering.

DIFFERENTIATING TYPES OF AGGRESSION

Fear-induced anxiety

When something in the dog's environment causes him to feel threatened, fearful and anxious, he might respond to this using aggression. Here, aggression is his natural form of communication, and it's used to tell the perceived threat to go away. The signs he will use can be very subtle at first, such as changes in posture or facial features. They may then progress to more obvious signs such as growling and snarling. If he feels the threat remains, he may launch into a physical attack.

Some anxious dogs will perceive threats in a vast array of different forms. These could include such seemingly innocuous things as a new object in the house or garden – an inflatable paddling pool, perhaps. Meeting new people out on a walk can also be perceived as a threatening situation, as can being in a situation with other dogs present. Some dogs will be frightened by anything thing that is new or unusual to their field of experience, and will seem to be aggressive pretty much all the time. This sort of fear-related aggression is common in dogs who had limited experiences in their puppyhoods. If the puppy was not introduced to a wide range of situations and experiences, then anything new will seem threatening to him as an adult dog. More confident and experienced dogs may show aggression in a narrower range of situations.

The fear-induced anxiety sufferer will appear to become anxious and aggressive in a range of different situations – he will be frightened of various different things. For some dogs, however, it is only very specific situations that trigger their fear-induced aggression. It may be that the dog is only aggressive toward children, or tall men. This is likely because he suffered bad treatment from the thing he is showing aggression toward (children played too roughly with him when he was little, or he was often physically punished by a tall man) and his associative memory is kicking in. The information in this chapter can still help with such a dog, but 'ASSOCIATIVE-MEMORY ANXIETY' (p185) should also prove useful.

When helping dogs who suffer from fear-induced anxiety and the subsequent aggression, the key thing we must remember is his behaviour is triggered by fear. He is frightened. We must not do anything to compound his fear. Remember: calm compassion.

Learned aggression

Most forms of aggression are a response induced by an external factor in the dog's environment which makes him feel he has no choice other than to become aggressive. Some dogs, however, initiate aggression themselves, with no prompting from an environmental factor, because they have learned that their aggressive behaviour gets them what they want. This learned aggression can also become a feature of dogs who have suffered fear-induced anxiety for some time without assistance in alleviating it.

For example, a dog suffering fear-induced anxiety may find human hands coming toward him (to stroke him, perhaps) a threat and respond with aggressive signs. Either he hasn't had much experience with human contact, or his has been physically abused in the past so his associative memory links the incoming hand with physical pain. His lips twitch, he growls, and when the hand still doesn't go away, he lashes out and bites. At last the hand withdraws and the dog begins to feel more secure. He has learned that being aggressive gets him what he wants (the hand going away; a sense of security) and is therefore encouraged to repeat the aggressive behaviour again. In order to promote his own personal sense of security, he may start taking the initiative and show aggression toward humans before they get the opportunity to thrust those horrifying hands toward him.

Learned aggression can also appear in dogs who have, in the quite literal sense, been taught to use aggression – unfortunate dogs who have been used in fighting, for example.

The way we handle learned aggression (which is detailed later) differs from fear-induced anxiety. This is because with the latter it is the underlying anxiety we need to address. Learned aggression can be employed by the dog when there is no anxiety; it is simply hard-wired into him as the first response. The aggression becomes impulsive rather than reactive. Therefore, it is the aggression itself, rather than the fear which causes it, that we need to address.

Genetic aggression

Some breeds of dog are predisposed toward aggressive behaviour; some dogs are selectively bred to draw out aggression.

Modern veterinary science does much to enhance our understanding of how aggressive tendencies are passed down bloodlines. For example, a study by Kathelijne Peremans, DVM, (p246) reveals that physical idiosyncrasies of the brain, such as abnormalities in the frontal cortex and temporal cortex, can promote the likelihood of a dog exhibiting impulsive aggressive behaviour. Irrespective of breed, such physical abnormality can be inherited allowing breeders to select dogs which exhibit the desired aggressive behaviour and pass it to their offspring.

Working with such dogs requires great patience and perseverance, as the aggressive tendencies are ingrained into them. Their impulsive aggression makes them feel as if they are performing the role they are inherently designed to fulfil, just as border collies get a kick out of herding. Therefore, owners are also faced with the ethical question – how fair is it to deprive the dog of his natural, inherent function?

Territorial aggression

Territorial aggression is when a dog wants to protect something which he deems is 'his', and which is threatened by an 'intruder'. The thing he wants to protect may be the house he lives in, his garden, some other part of 'his' territory, or it may be people such as yourself or a family member. The 'intruder' may well be an actual intruder (in which case, good boy!) but it's just as likely to be an innocuous visitor to your house, a dog and walker passing by the back fence, or even a blackbird landing in the garden.

The protective dog's intention is to frighten off the perceived intruder. He doesn't want to fight with or hurt the intruder, and won't do so unless the intruder persists in the invasion of the dog's territory. The intention to frighten means that territorial aggression is a very noisy affair, which certainly makes it undesirable for the surrounding humans.

Territorial aggression can easily become a learned form of aggression. Most people won't hang around when the protective dog is manically warning them away, teeth slashing and saliva flying.

When they back off, the dog has got what he wants, and will learn to repeat the behaviour.

Territorial aggression is usually indicative of a leadership identity crisis. The dog feels the territory, possession or person he protects belongs to him. It usually occurs in dogs who have assumed a leader position in the owner/dog relationship. We need to establish ourselves back in the position of leader, and reassert ourselves as master and owner of the dog's territory. This will give him the comfort and security of knowing it is someone else's job to do the protecting. We'll look at ways to alleviate territorial aggression later in this chapter, but you should also consult the chapter on 'LEADERSHIP ANXIETY'.

Pack aggression

Also known as social aggression or dominance aggression, pack aggression is seen when a dog behaves aggressively toward other members of his pack. This could be other dogs in the household, or yourself, or other family members.

Pack aggression tends to occur in dogs who are used to assuming a leadership/parental position in their pack, and are reluctant to surrender this position. This can cause aggressive behaviour when an owner wants the dog to do something he isn't keen on, such as getting of the sofa, or wants to take something away from the dog, such as an object he shouldn't be chewing. The dog sees himself as leader and protests when an 'inferior' member of the hierarchy imposes authority.

It can be common in dogs who spent much of their puppyhood with their siblings, and assumed a dominant role during this time. It is perhaps less common in puppies who are separated from their pack at eight weeks, the typical sort of time a new owner will take the puppy away from the breeder. However, pack aggression can still manifest in such a puppy if he is treated rather indulgently. If the puppy gets to sleep wherever he wants, gets treats for doing nothing, and is otherwise spoiled by his owner, then he will grow into a dog who thinks he has free access rights to whatever he wants. He's essentially claiming the primary, dominant position in the 'pack', which is why this is called pack aggression.

Because of his self-determined aleadership position, the dog will likely be keen to keep other dogs in the pack firmly in line. He'll try to take their food and snap at them if they protest, he'll get snarly if the owner shows another dog attention over him, he'll generally do his best to impose a rigid totalitarian regime upon the pack.

Clearly, he needs to be shown who is the true leader of the pack. We'll look at the right ways to do this later in the chapter; 'LEADERSHIP ANXIETY' will also help.

Resource guarding

This is a form of aggression which manifests in some dogs when they feel something in their possession, e.g. a bone, is going to be taken away from them. When the owner's hand approaches the dog to remove the bone, it may come away with a few teeth marks in it and probably no bone. The resource guarder may also show aggression toward other dogs who threaten his possession over the desired object.

It is difficult to know why some dogs are aggressive resource guarders, and others are not. Some theories propose that it is an inherited trait. It can also be a learned experience. A puppy will scour the house looking for interesting things he can test out in his mouth and on his teeth; the conscientious owner will quickly retrieve the object. The puppy will learn to run away next time he finds something interesting, so the conscientious owner follows and again repossesses the object. When this little cat-and-mouse process is repeated, the puppy may well resort to aggression. He's tried running off, but that didn't work, and he knows no other way to keep that pesky human hand away from his precious treasure. Unfortunately, this probably will work. The owner will back off, and the pup learns his aggressive behaviour gets him what he wants.

We can help a resource guarder by developing his understanding that any food, toy or other object is given to him by his master; they are not for him to claim ownership over. We'll look at how to do this the right way later in the chapter.

Pain-induced aggression

Finally, we must remember that sometimes aggressive behaviour, especially if it has a sudden onset, may be due physical pain or illness suffered by the dog. He has a heightened sense of vulnerability, and his defences are understandably sharp. Sometimes the source of pain won't be obvious, and reading a book isn't going to help – he needs to be checked over by a vet!

AGGRESSION QUIZ

The particular nature of a dog's aggression isn't always obvious. What type of aggression do you think each dog is suffering in the following case studies? Answers are at the back of the book.

1) *Every morning the postman comes at about nine o'clock while my dog and I are watching television. As soon as my dog hears the sound of the front gate opening, he is up on his feet, dashing toward the door, barks shaking the walls and saliva splattering all over them. He attacks the mail when it appears through the letterbox.*

2) *Every morning the postman comes at about nine o'clock while my dog and I are watching television. As soon as my dog hears the sound of the front gate opening, he starts licking his lips. When he hears the postman's footsteps approaching up the drive, he starts growling. The growls get louder and louder. He attacks the mail when it appears through the letterbox.*

3) *I have three dogs who eat dinner together. At meal time yesterday, one of my dogs, Bingo, spilled some of his biscuits onto the floor while he was eating from his bowl. One of the other dogs tried to grab them, but got his ear bitten by Bingo who snapped viciously at him.*

4) *My dog and I are out for a nice quiet walk in the woods; he is off the lead. Another dog appears, no owner in sight, and comes wandering over to us. This dog and my dog sniff each other for a bit, both tails stuck high in the air. I'm a bit worried about this other dog and want to move away, so I put my own dog back on the lead. Suddenly my dog starts growling, which makes the other dog growl too. It looks as if things are really going to kick off.*

5) *My obedience instructor told me it's really important to give my dog a regular health inspection by examining his teeth, feet, ears, skin, etc. However, whenever I try to do this my dog snaps at me. I'm really worried, because not only have I been unable to check my dog for any problems, but it must also mean we have a really bad relationship if he doesn't like to be touched!*

6) *My husband goes out to work in the evenings and my dog gets really upset when he leaves the house; she'll scrabble at the door trying to follow him. Eventually she'll calm down, and will relax on my lap while we sit on the sofa watching a film. But when my husband gets home a few hours later and enters the living room, my dog starts growling. The* *growls get louder when my husband moves closer, and my dog gets really snappy if my husband actually tries to move her from the sofa.*

AGGRESSION: THE WARNING SIGNS

One thing we must be really alert to when helping dogs overcome their aggressive tendencies is the generous quantity of warning signs they offer. Because some of these are subtle, many owners are quite late in recognising that their dog's behaviour is becoming aggressive, only becoming aware with the more obvious, later signs such as growling and snarling which often preface an imminent attack.

The pictures in this section are available in the public domain and were not taken by the author. No dogs were put into stressful situations for the sake of this book.

1) Licking.

Licking of the lips or nose is one of the first signs a dog may exhibit when an environmental factor triggers his anxiety. If a dog perceives a threat, he may lick his lips in an attempt to appease that threat – to show that he himself has no aggressive intention toward the threat. Licking of the nose tends to be what is known as a displacement sign – a dog who perceives a threat licks his nose to distract the attention of the threat. The dog is trying to make the threat focus on his action of licking his nose, rather than on the dog himself. Sniffing, sneezing and shaking (as if trying to get water off his coat) are other examples of displacement signs.

In both cases, licking is clearly non-aggressive behaviour, but it is a sign that the dog is anxious due to a perceived threat. If the dog feels the threat persists, he may escalate into aggressive behaviour.

You can see in the above picture that the dog is not too happy about having such a close-up photo taken. The camera, so close to him, is making him feel vulnerable and so he tries to distract attention from his self with the action of licking his nose. The whites of his eyes are also showing, which is further evidence of his anxiety (see below).

2) Yawning.

Yawning is also a very early sign, and doesn't always indicate that the dog is feeling threatened. It is another displacement sign, a bit like nose licking, but rather than distracting the focus of an external threat, the dog uses it to distract his own internal feeling of stress. It makes him feel better.

You might see it when the dog is feeling threatened, but it might also just indicate that he is in a state of anticipation. For example, if you're out walking but you stop to talk to a passer-by, you might notice your dog yawning. He's keen to continue walking, and yawns to distract himself from his anticipatory feelings. Or, if something a bit unusual is happening at home, such as you rooting about in all the kitchen drawers for some keys you've mislaid, your dog might become alert and start yawning. He feels like something is about to happen (are we going out for a walk? Is he getting me some food?) but he's not sure what, and yawning helps distract himself from this insecurity.

So we need to be sensitive to the context. If we're out for a walk, and a strange dog approaches, your dog's yawn could well signify he is trying to calm some rising feelings of anxiety that could escalate into aggressive behaviour. (Or he might just be tired.)

3) Turning the head away.

This is an appeasement gesture. If a dog perceives a threat, he may turn his head away from the threat to show he has no aggressive intentions and doesn't wish to engage in conflict.

The young man in the picture above is probably just trying to show his dog some attention. However, he's failing to recognise the sign of anxiety in his dog who is going to great efforts to turn his head away. The dog is feeling stressed and threatened by the man's intensity. With his appeasement gesture he is doing his best to show the man that he does not wish to engage in conflict. Let's hope things didn't escalate.

4) Weight on the rear legs.

This is a useful early-warning sign to watch for. Notice how the dog in the picture has his body tucked back, so his rear legs are very vertical. It looks as if he has perceived something which might be deemed a threat, and is thinking about taking flight. This is another appeasement sign. If he is forced to continue toward the threat (for example, if he were on a lead and his owner insisted he continue forward), this may escalate into aggressive behaviour.

5) Whites of the eyes showing.

This can be a sign that the dog's anxiety is escalating and he may be getting closer to aggressive behaviour. When a dog turns his head away from a perceived threat in an attempt to appease, but feels so anxious that he doesn't want to take his eyes off the threat, the whites of his eyes will show. We can see this happening in the picture above. The head turns away, but the eyes remain fixed on the threat, with whites clearly showing. He is trying to remain non-confrontational, but the eye contact signifies his increasing anxiety.

6) Ears.

I don't think the dog in this picture is very happy about having his photograph taken. His mouth is firmly closed, which suggests he isn't relaxed. His eyes are fixed and staring, which in a context of anxiety suggests the dog is moving from a non-confrontational to a confrontational attitude. Furthermore, his ears are held low, tensed, and toward the back of his head. This sort of visible tension is a clear sign that the dog's anxiety is increasing, and he is moving toward offensive behaviour.

7) Tails.

It can be useful to keep an eye on your dog's tail when he is entering a social situation – with other dogs or people.

If his tail is high in the air and stiff, he is probably feeling confident. He is allowing the scent from his anal glands to be emitted, showing he is comfortable to communicate with other dogs.

A slowly wagging tail often signifies that your dog is not yet sure about the situation he is entering into. He is still judging it, and is not fully confident. Look out for further signs which might indicate his final judgement.

A tail which is really going for it – wagging widely and rapidly, or going round in circles, speaks of a happy, excited dog – a good sign!

If your dog's tail is hanging lowly, perhaps between his legs, it may well signify his lack of confidence. This is probably a sign that anxiety is building.

Another tail-related sign of an anxious dog are non-wagging tails which extend stiffly from the dog's rear end, and curve upwards. This is a tense tail, and one that speaks of the dog's defensive attitude.

8) Other warning signs.

A lowered body, or a body which drops to the ground, is a clear appeasement sign which your dog uses to show others he is being non-confrontational. A lowered head and rolling over onto the back are also appeasement signs. This sounds like a good thing – your 'aggressive' dog is demonstrating that he wants to be non-confrontational, but these signs also mean he thinks he has perceived a possible threat and is feeling uncertain. His behaviour may escalate quickly. Other signs of a stressed, possibly soon-to-be-aggressive dog include jaw and facial tension, rigid eye contact, and raised hair down the spine.

How things escalate

If your dog has done his best to appease, distract, and show his non-confrontational attitude, but he decides the perceive threat is still a threat, he will enter confrontational, offensive, aggressive mode. This will likely begin with a tense body whose weight is on the front legs, growling with wobbling lips, and sharp, resolute eye contact on the perceived threat.

In other situations, the escalation might be something like a warning snap at the perceived threat. This will involve dental contact, but the dog won't hold on. The purpose of it is to warn rather than harm.

If the dog still feels the threat is unabated, he will lash out again with a deeper bite, holding on this time. He may shake his head violently. This is a not-too-subtle 'sign' that he's fed up with trying to patiently warn the threat away – he wants to hurt and possibly kill it.

The power of warning signs

If all, or some, of the above signs appear in your dog when he's confronted by a strange and aggressive dog, we would have every sympathy for him entering attack mode. But remember he can perceive an equal threat to the one presented by the strange aggressive dog in anything – whether it be a playful little lapdog yapping at his ankles, or even an inquisitive child.

Whether training, or out in real-world situations, we always need to be keeping a sharp eye out for the earliest appearance of warning signs.

There's a fascinating video on YouTube in which a news reporter is interviewing a police dog handler. The handler's German Shepherd is also in front of the camera, between interviewer and handler, being casually stroked by the interviewer. They are all crouched low on the ground, so the dog's head is close to the handler's and interviewer's.

Presumably because he is so focused on the questions being asked of him, the handler misses several warning signs which indicate the German Shepherd has perceived the interviewer as a threat and his anxiety is subsequently rising.

The dog's head is turned sharply away from the interviewer in a gesture of appeasement. Shortly into the video, the dog licks his lips in another attempt to appease the perceived threat. The interviewer keeps stroking. Then the dog turns his head to make eye contact with the interviewer − a sign that he is shifting from appeasement to confrontation. Neither the interviewer or the handler notice his changing behaviour. Moments later, the dog lashes out and bites the interviewer on the head. It's a warning, non-holding bite. To the untrained viewer, the dog suddenly becomes aggressive. But we were able to recognise the dog's signs; we understood the dog was suffering fear-induced anxiety long before he actually became aggressive, and we could have prevented several tooth marks from marring a TV personality's forehead.

AGGRESSIVE DOG: WHAT *NOT* TO DO

Let's use a hypothetical scenario to explore the wrong approaches for helping an aggressive dog.

I am out walking my dog in the forest; he is on the lead. A jogger is approaching us along the path from the opposite direction. This jogger is wearing high-visibility fluorescent clothing. Because I'm in a world of my own day dreams, I neglect to register that the sight of this fast-approaching, alarmingly kaleidoscopic jogger might trigger my dog's anxiety. I'm also oblivious to my dog's early warning signs – the stiff, curved tail, the nose licking, the hard eye contact fixed on the jogger, and the raised hair on his spine. As the jogger comes past, my dog lashes out and tries to snap at him.

My immediate reaction is to jerk hard on the lead and admonish in a loud, angry voice. This is punishment. The jerk on the lead causes him physical pain (and possibly harm); the verbal admonishment frightens him when he is already feeling frightened by the perceived threat. He will associate the feeling of anxiety he experienced from the perceived threat with the pain and fear subjected to him by me, the owner, and next time a jogger appears his defensive behaviour will be all the more virulent.

And why should he be punished? What has he done wrong? He's only behaved in the way nature instructs. The only individual who's done anything wrong is me. I failed to read the signs my dog was trying to communicate. So let's go back in time to look at an alternative approach.

The jogger is running toward us on the forest path. My dog gives an obvious sign that he has perceived the jogger as a threat: he growls. I am horrified and a bit embarrassed that the jogger might have heard my dog growling at him, so I verbally admonish the dog and give him a jerk on the lead or tap on the nose to let him know that growling is wrong.

But it's not wrong! Growling is a perfectly natural and appropriate way for a dog to respond to something that frightens him. To me, the owner, it seems wrong because he's growling at an innocent jogger, but it's not the dog's fault that he finds this frightening any more than it is arachnophobia sufferers' 'fault' for being frightened of spiders. If he were growling at a burglar robbing my house, I'd be perfectly fine with it. But in the dog's anxiety-fuelled perception, there is no difference between the burglar and jogger.

With my punishment I have not only been unjust, but I have taught him his feelings of fear will be punished – making future fearful experiences more frightening, which will increase his defensiveness. Let's try again.

The jogger is running toward us on the path. I am alert to my dog's signals, and I understand he has perceived the jogger as a threat. I know my dog's warning signs are likely to escalate into real aggression toward the jogger. I have to avert the encounter, so I get my dog out of there. I take him down a side path, or bash our way through the brambles; I do whatever it takes to get him away from the area before the jogger reaches us.

This is certainly a better approach. I have prevented the escalation into aggression, and ensured no harm, beyond a few bramble scratches, comes to anyone. However, this hasn't help my dog overcome his underlying anxiety of the perceived threat. Next time we meet a jogger, my dog will still respond in the same fear-induced way. Also, running's quite popular these days and there are lots of joggers about – I can't go prancing off into the bushes every time we see one. Try again.

The jogger is running toward us. I become alert to my dog's warning signs. I want to help him overcome his anxiety. So I get down on my knees, give him a big fuss and a few treats, I keep saying 'who's a good boy?' and give him lots of reassuring strokes. My dog's still focused on the jogger so I start getting desperate, increasing the fervour of my strokes and pretty much force the treats into his mouth. 'Who's a good boy?' I frantically plead again, but it's no good – the jogger comes past and my dog tries to snap at him.

Why didn't it work? This is the 'molly-coddle' approach. When we sense our dogs are anxious, we try to soothe and calm them, just as I do here with the jogger. The trouble with molly-coddling is that it confirms my dog's suspicion that something is wrong. My sudden change in behaviour is a clear sign that I am worried about something. My dog easily picks up on my own anxiety, which validates his anxiety and encourages him to react to it with aggression. Try again.

Here comes the jogger. I know this might trigger my dog's anxiety, and I anticipate his warning signs before they even appear. Sure enough, he starts nose licking/growling/drooping his tail. Don't panic. I immediately ensure I am exuding an air of confidence. I stand tall and straight; I want him to feed off my own confidence. I also don't want to confirm his suspicions that anything is wrong, so I don't change the tension on my dog's lead, I don't alter our walking pace, and I don't say anything to mollify him. I whip out one of the aggressive-dog owner's secret weapons, the clicker, and get some treats ready. I calmly ask my dog to 'heel'. This isn't unusual for him; we often practise it, so it's not going to compound his anxiety. In fact, obeying my request gives him the sense of comfort and security provided by clear leadership. I reward his correct heeling by clicking and treating. His attention's on me, because he's waiting to be rewarded for his good behaviour. Sure enough, at fairly generous intervals, I click and treat his good heeling. If his attention wavers from me, I simply ask him to 'heel' again, and click and treat when he complies. At some point during all this, the jogger blithely trotted past. My dog was too focused on his own heeling/treat affairs to notice exactly when.

So which is the best approach? The last one? I disagree. In a controlled environment it would absolutely be the best. I was able to use my own confidence and leadership to give my dog a sense of security, waylaying his anxiety, and cemented this by using the clicker and our good training habits with lots of positive reinforcement. I will have helped my dog feel less anxious the next time a similar anxiety trigger arises. The trouble is, this wasn't a controlled situation. I could not be sure that my dog wouldn't lash out at the jogger, so I was putting that person in jeopardy. The best approach in this uncontrolled context was the one where I took my dog out of the situation before it could even develop.

Summing up

The hypothetical jogger has shown us a few things about the right and wrong ways to approach anxiety-fuelled aggression.

- o We can't punish. This is unfair and just makes our dogs' anxiety more severe.

- o Molly-coddling doesn't work because it validates the dog's anxiety rather than alleviates it.

- o Practice has to occur in a controlled way. We can't subject our dogs to any situations where failure is likely, or where the safety of others might be jeopardised. We can't force him too far out of his comfort zone too soon.

- o Aggressive behaviour cannot be effectively tackled without the support of a good training regime, and the clicker is an important tool to make this optimally effective.

- o We have to control ourselves before we can hope to control our dogs. We need to exude the calm confidence we want him to share.

- o Always carry treats.

Another word about punishment

Let's think about punishment in a different context. You enter your bedroom and turn the light on to find your dog luxuriantly sprawled across your nice clean duvet. You don't want him to be there so you stomp toward him and yell, 'GET OFF!'. You just want to send a clear message. But this is punishment, whether by accident or design. The loud admonishment and physical show of force frighten your dog. How is he going to react?

A: He thinks, 'Hmm…this loud-mouthed person seems to be upset. I wonder why? Is he frightened of something? Is he feeling unwell? Or could it be something to do with me innocently enjoying this lovely comfy spot? Let's see…I suppose the logical thing for me to do would be to climb off this bed, and then he might not be so upset. I'll try doing that.'

Or

B: He thinks, 'this angry man is frightening me I'm going to bark and snap at him!!'

It's not hard to determine the more dog-like thought process. Dogs are reactive creatures. They act on impulse and instinct rather than thinking things through. Any aggression shown toward them is asking for reactive aggression in return. Our aim should be to alleviate aggression, not stimulating more through accidental or purposeful punishment.

VITAL APPROACHES

There are several very important approaches we need to adopt when helping a dog overcome his aggressive tendencies:

- o   A training regimen

- o Leadership

- o Modelling

- o Control

- o Exercise

Each of these is vital, no matter what type of aggression the dog is suffering.

A training regimen

We need to go all 'boot camp' on the dog. You are the drill sergeant (a calm, compassionate one); he is the squaddie. Every morning or evening we go out into the garden and, rather than doing fifty push-ups, practise commands such as 'sit', 'down', 'stay', and sometimes train something new.

The 'boot camp' analogy is perhaps not quite fitting, as this shouldn't involve the owner intimidating the dog or putting the dog through something he's not enjoying. Imagine a squaddie who really loves push-ups and wants to work with his drill sergeant to get the very best ones – that's your dog.

Your training sessions are cooperative and reciprocal, always focused on **fun** and **positive reinforcement**. Your dog loves them because they give him good mental stimulation, a generous amount of treats as rewards, and –perhaps most importantly – they cement a bond of trust and understanding between him and his owner. He builds confidence in your leadership. This will be vital to him when you start taking him out in real-world situations where his anxiety might be triggered. If he's more confident, trusting and understanding in you, the strength of those anxieties will be greatly diminished.

This training needs to be regular and habitual. Some owners might think they've already accomplished it, because many moons ago they taught their dog to do a 'sit' and 'down'. But it's not something that can be 'finished'; the owner needs to make it a regular, ongoing part of the dog's life.

It should happen in a place where your dog feels comfortable, so if his anxieties are likely to be triggered in the garden, do it indoors. Start doing it with your dog in his crate if necessary; wherever he feels calm and confident. Over time, you'll be able to take him further out of his old comfort zone.

For training to give the most efficient, rapid improvement in our dogs' behaviour, we are going to need the aggressive-dog owner's **secret weapon no.1**: the clicker. A clicker is a small handheld device with a button. When your dog does something good, you press this button. The clicker makes a 'click' noise. This tells your dog (in clearer terms than our verbal praise can achieve) that he has done something right. He is given a treat immediately after the click. He will want to repeat the same behaviour in order to elicit another 'click' and treat.

Owners who use clickers have a far, far easier time helping their dogs overcome aggressive tendencies. The clicker is likely to help a dog who is so anxious that training has been otherwise impossible. They are available from pet shops for only a couple of pounds/dollars. Get one right away, then refer to the 'CLICKER' section (p234) in the 'TRAINING' chapter, which explains how to teach the dog what the clicker means; this must be done before the clicker can exert its beneficial effect.

Once your dog is attuned to the clicker, you can start your daily training routine. Keep sessions short and enjoyable, and try to do them at the same time each day – the routine will help your dog's sense of security.

Some good first things to teach include reinforcing your dog's name, simple commands like 'sit' and 'down', and the ever-useful 'settle' (see p233). Even if your dog already knows these, reinforce them with the clicker.

Carry your clicker (and treats) with you wherever you and your dog go – we'll be using it in shaping positive responses to anxiety-inducing stimuli.

Make sure you enrol your dog and yourself in a regular training/obedience class. There are lots of these about, and you should find you don't have to travel far. The one I use is a fifteen-minute drive away and costs £5 for each one-hour session. Use the internet to find one with proper certification. When you enrol, discuss your dog's aggressive tendencies. The instructors will be really supportive and will help your dog socialise safely. My class often gets new members who are really anxious dogs and who show aggression. An instructor works with the dog and owner individually in a separate room for the first few sessions. Then they start introducing the dog, gradually, to the main room. It is great to see the burgeoning confidence in these dogs.

Leadership

Because dogs are social creatures, and inherently pack orientated, anxiety and aggression can be compounded if they don't have a clear understanding or respect for your position as leader or parent.

Fear-induced anxiety is going to be worsened if the dog can't trust his leader's confidence in stressful contexts – worsened too if he's not sure whether it's the owner or himself who is fulfilling the leader/parent role. Other types of aggression, such as pack aggression or resource guarding, are very often compounded because the dog assumes a leader/parent position. This is not his fault; it's not because of his dominance. It's because we, the owners, haven't managed to effectively assert our leadership role.

Some owners have a fantastically harmonious relationship with their very peaceful dogs, but are in fact woeful leaders. They can lounge next to their dogs on the sofas, share their bed with their dog, share their food, etc. It all sounds lovely, but it's letting the dog know that he has equal status as the owner. If they have equal status, then who exactly is the leader? Some owners get away with this because their dogs are calm, confident and placid. But it's not going to fly for the dog prone to anxiety. He needs – wants – to know that his owner bears the responsibility of clear leadership. Therefore, the following chapter on 'LEADERSHIP ANXIETY' is required reading for any owner looking to help his dog overcome aggression – no matter what variety of aggression. That chapter explores how to assert our role as leader in the right ways – positive, non punitive ways that aren't going to intimidate the dog, but make him feel more secure and happy in his pack.

Modelling

Imagine going on an organised expedition through the Amazon jungle with a group leader who doesn't seem to know what he's doing. He keeps pausing to try and figure out which way he should be going, he starts nervously at every movement in the bushes, he can't give accurate answers to your insightful questions about the local flora and fauna. It makes you much more nervous than if you had a guide who confidently scythed a path through the undergrowth, showing no fear of the snakes that slither out of his way. You're going to get to the uncomfortable point where you feel you ought to take charge instead.

It's the same experience for the dog whose owner is an ineffective leader. The context might be the dog park instead of the

Amazon jungle, but he's still going to feed off your insecurities. We must always make sure we are exuding confidence and calm, because we are modelling (whether we realise it or not) the behaviour we want our dogs to follow. And they are remarkably adept at picking up on our own attitudes.

But don't fully dismiss your own insecurity. If you are entering a situation where you are finding it hard to keep your nerves calm, it probably means that deep down you are aware of putting your dog into too extreme a situation. Be alert to this possibility, and be prepared to pull out if you feel you might be setting your dog up for failure.

Control

We need to keep tight control over the situations we thrust our dogs into. If he has a fear-induced aggression triggered by anxiety of strange dogs, we're not going to immediately leap into the local park's dog pen, hoping that our clicker and treats will get us through. Very gradually widening our dogs' comfort zones is the way to go, and we monitor this by being really alert to our dogs' warning signs.

'Control' also means making sure our dogs and others are always safe. This means using a muzzle and halter lead. Some dogs will be reluctant to wear these at first, so we use the clicker to train his comfort. See 'WEARING A MUZZLE' (p239) in the 'TRAINING' chapter.

Exercise

Nothing too revolutionary here, but it's nevertheless hugely important that our dogs get plenty of exercise. A deficiency means he is not getting the stimulation and endorphins needed for a happy, healthy, fulfilled dog. He is going to have lots of pent up energy which will fuel his anxieties and aggressive tendencies.

Good exercise needs to involve free running off the lead, which can be tricky to do safely for a dog prone to aggression. Be prepared to travel some distance to find the right place. If you haven't got a big garden, find a friend or neighbour who has. Proper obedience classes can be great here, because they often have large fenced-off enclosures where your dog can freely and safely run. Other dogs can be introduced to this space in a controlled, professionally supervised manner.

Training, leadership, modelling, control and exercise – these are our fundamental, non-skippable approaches for helping dogs overcome aggression. Now we'll go on to look at more specific methods for different types of aggression.

METHODS: FEAR-INDUCED ANXIETY

Remember, with fear-induced aggression we're dealing with dogs who get anxious and then aggressive in any general situation outside of their comfort zone. If your dog becomes anxious or aggressive only in response to very specific triggers – certain types of people or a specific place – then 'ASSOCIATIVE-MEMORY ANXIETY' (p185) will be much more helpful.

Conditioning

We're going to start by employing two key techniques: 'conditioning' and 'operant conditioning'. Conditioning involves making the dog feel more comfortable in a context where he would normally experience signs of anxiety. Operant conditioning involves rewarding the dog for his own actions and behaviour.

To explore how these techniques work, we'll use an example dog: Alfred.

Alfred

Poor old Alfred: he's generally comfortable indoors, but when he is taken outside, into the garden, he gets frightened and becomes defensive. He growls at sounds and movements in the garden, shows aggressive signs to people or dogs that pass by outside the garden, and even occasionally snaps at his owner because his anxiety is so high. Alfred might have this fear-induced anxiety because he only had a very sheltered puppyhood and upbringing; he wasn't introduced to new places and experiences. Or he might be a recently rehomed animal from a rescue shelter.

Alfred is quite fortunate, in a sense, because at least he has his indoor comfort zone. Some dogs won't even have that, and will feel anxious/aggressive wherever they are. We'll look at such an extreme case after Alfred.

We are going to use conditioning and operant conditioning to turn Alfred into a dog who is not only confident and comfortable in his garden, but out on walks too.

We have already worked on Alfred's training regimen, indoors where he feels safe, so he responds to the clicker and can perform basic commands indoors.

While he is indoors, and feeling reasonably secure, we put his lead and muzzle on. This is important because once we progress to real-world situations, out in the park etc., he will need to be accustomed to wearing these. At first, it was difficult to get him comfortable wearing them, but we followed the guidance under 'WEARING A MUZZLE' (p239).

With him fully dressed, we ask Alfred to 'heel' and begin leading Alfred toward the back door. We use our leadership and modelling to let Alfred share our confidence, but we also keep a sharp eye on him to watch for the first signs of anxiety. Because he knows 'heel' – we have trained it indoors – Alfred's attention is on us at first, waiting for his clicks and treats to reward his nice heeling. But as we get close to the back door, his eye contact switches from us and remains fixed on the door. That is the first warning sign of anxiety.

It's at this point we start 'conditioning'. We have left Alfred's comfort zone, and are on the periphery of the anxiety zone. We want to help him feel calm and confident rather than anxious, and we need to start right on the edge of the anxiety zone, therefore we don't move any closer to the door once his first anxiety sign has appeared. We use leadership and positive reinforcement to help him feel confident in this place on the edge of his anxiety zone.

Keeping our voice, posture and general demeanour calm and confident, we ask Alfred to 'sit'. When he obeys, we click and treat. Then we ask him to stand 'up', again clicking and treating. We can give lots of verbal praise, too, and a good fussing. If we judge Alfred is able to handle it, we might ask for another sit, or a down, or other exercise we know he is able to do. Then we take him away from the door, back into his comfort zone.

What just happened and how does it help?

1. We established the edge of Alfred's comfort zone, which is also the start of his anxiety zone. For Alfred, this was about three feet away from the back door that leads out into the garden.

2. We used conditioning to begin to replace Alfred's very soonest feelings of anxiety with feelings of security and pleasure. He

gets the security by following our commands, feeling the confidence of being under safe leadership. He gets the pleasure from the rewards, and from our verbal praise and fussing. He starts to feel more secure on the edge of his comfort zone, and we can begin work on widening his comfort zone very gradually.

What can go wrong?

1. **Alfred gets aggressive.** We have pushed him too far out of his comfort zone; we didn't notice his warning signs or he didn't exhibit them. Next time (a few hours later or the next day) we don't push him so far, and we watch closely for his subtle anxiety warning signs. It is also possible, if this has been a repeating pattern, that his aggressive behaviour here is learned aggression. If Alfred has discovered that begin aggressive stops his owner from leading him outside his comfort zone, then he has learned to produce the behaviour and it may not be accompanied by warning signs.

2. **Alfred doesn't sit when we tell him to.** He may be a bit too far outside his comfort zone, or he needs more reinforcement of 'sit'. So we go back to training 'sit' deep within his comfort zone.

3. **It works, but Alfred hardly seems calm when he sits.** No, but he will become more calm on subsequent practices. It takes time for the associations to shift – he is going from associating the edge of his comfort zone with a feeling of anxiety, to a feeling of confidence and pleasure; this isn't going to be immediate.

Look at an aerial view of Alfred's comfort and anxiety zones:

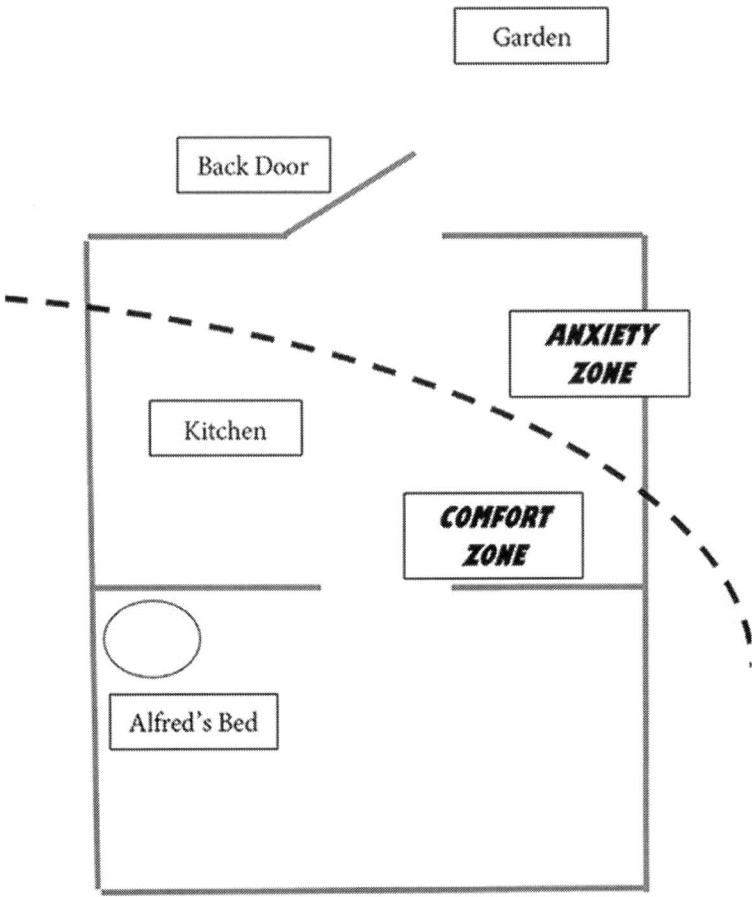

The dashed line shows the point where Alfred first showed anxiety signs, and where we asked him to sit and stand up, giving lots of positive reinforcement. We began 'conditioning' him to associate this place with a confident, pleasurable feeling. We'll need to do quite a lot of reinforcement of this, so we go through the same exercise a few hours later or the next day. We might add a couple of different commands to condition his confidence on the anxiety-zone border, provided we know he can obey them easily.

Now we can use 'operant conditioning' to help stretch Alfred's comfort zone. Operant conditioning is when we reward the dog for good behaviour – we've already been using it with Alfred, to reward his good heeling as we lead him toward the door with the clicker and treats.

Next time we lead Alfred toward the edge of his comfort zone, we aim to keep his attention on us while heeling for a bit longer before he gets distracted by anxiety. When his first anxiety warning sign appears, we stop and condition, but hopefully this will be a bit further than last time. If not, we just reinforce and try again next time.

That's how we stretch his comfort zone. Let's see what progress might look like over the course of several days:

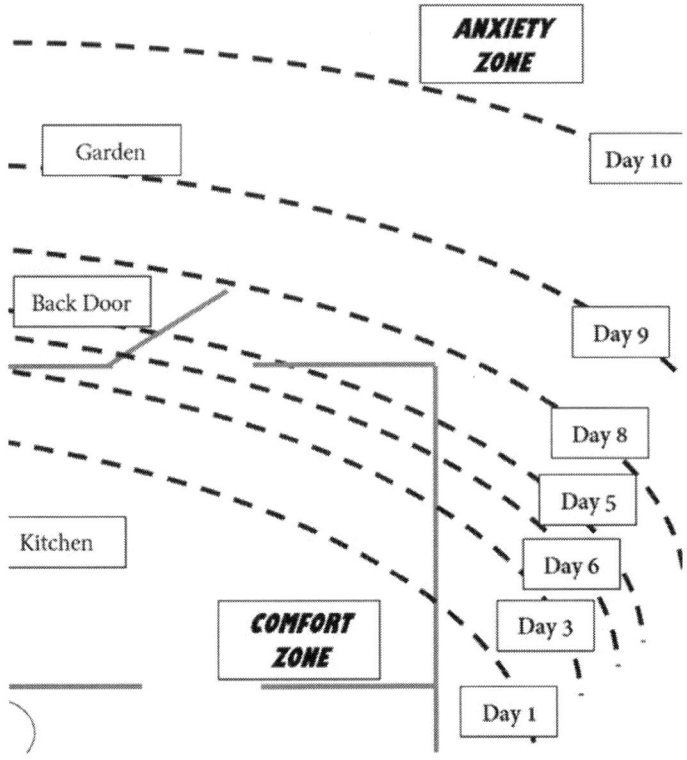

Notice that to begin with there are gaps of one or two days between progression – this is because we reinforce on the intervening days. There was a slight setback on day 6 – we pushed Alfred too soon, or he heard a dog barking which triggered his anxiety. No problem; we just reinforce for the next day, and then try pushing again.

The gaps between days start becoming shorter and progression becomes exponentially greater, which is the normal course of things. It's the early stages which we want to take really slowly.

Alfred does really well here – he's feeling confident out in his garden after just ten days. Many dogs will need the comfort-zone stretching process to be much slower, with longer intervals of reinforcement between progression days.

Once he's happy in the garden, we can stretch further by taking him out of the garden, introducing him to the car, driving to the park, gradually stretching his comfort zone using the same approach.

Molly

With Molly, we've got a rather more extreme case of fear-induced aggression. Molly is so anxious of everything that she doesn't even have a comfort zone. When in the house, she finds it impossible to rest, destroys furniture, and withdraws from her owners or lashes out at them.

Dogs can't persist in this state for long without finding *somewhere* they at least feel a little protected. **We wait for Molly to find this place; it's not something we can choose for her.** In the meantime, we do our best to keep her and ourselves safe from harm.

Eventually, Molly seems to settle in a little niche under the sink in the utility room. This tiny little spot, only a few square inches, is her comfort zone – the only place in her world where she feels remotely secure. And even here, she is far from being entirely confident, but it's all she's got. Any attempt to approach Molly while she's in her comfort zone results in her lashing out at us – she is frightened of us, and responds to her anxiety with defensive aggression.

We put her food and water close enough that she can access them, but not so close we risk injury. Same goes for newspaper she can use as a toilet. We don't make the mistake of thinking Molly will be happier if we shut the utility room door. We need to be able to access it, and the sudden shock of having the door to her little world opened will be tremendously stressful. So we keep it open all the time.

Before we can even think about stretching Molly's comfort zone, we have to be able to include ourselves in it. We need to approach her without seeming to approach her, and condition her to trust us in her comfort zone.

So, we go about our daily affairs, seemingly oblivious to Molly's frightened little existence under the utility sink. We avoid looking at her; we certainly don't speak to her or engage with her in any way. Sometimes, however, our daily affairs are going to require our entry to the utility room, which means approaching her space. Perhaps we need to fetch a broom, or wipe some marks off the walls.

When we do this, we don't enter her space too intrusively — we remain on the edge, just coming into the corner of the utility room. But we still **don't look** at or speak to her, even to mollify her. We will likely detect some anxiety warning signs from Molly — growling, for example. This is okay; we ignore them completely and just continue with our private business, showing no response to her signs. If we back off when she makes them, she is going to learn that her aggression gets the desired response. We want to show her there is no need for aggression, or anxiety.

So long as we keep ignoring Molly and her warning signs, she will start to realise there is no need to be alarmed by our presence. It may take a long time to get to this point. We might find we can get a bit further into her space before the warning signs appear, so we push a bit further but ensure we are not risking her lashing out at us. Gently does it. Occasionally we'll drop a couple of treats on the floor — note, we don't 'give' them to her, because we're still in the non-engagement stage. As far as Molly's concerned, she thinks we don't know she even exists. But the treats help to condition her to our presence in her space. She starts to welcome our entry into her space, because she associates it with the arrival of some nice treats.

Slowly, we work our way into her space using this conditioning approach. Eventually we can wander about in the utility room without any warning signs. We still don't engage with her, though.

Something I like to do at this point is sit down in the room, perhaps leaning against the wall opposite Molly's comfort zone, and read a book. By showing her that I am in her presence but my attention is not on her, I help her feel unthreatened. If I look at her, she might feel suddenly under threat. So I keep my attention firmly on my book, turning pages occasionally even if I'm not really reading it, to show it is occupying my attention. Sometimes I might (seemingly haphazardly) knock a couple of treats her way – always without looking.

When Molly seems comfortable with this, we start watching for her first signs of engagement. This is when she shows non-anxious (or aggressive) interest in us. This is likely to be in the form of her watching us in a relaxed way – no tensed ears or jaw. If her head is cocked sideways a bit, that's a good sign of relaxed interest. Of course, we can't actually look at her directly ourselves, so we try to use our periphery vision to spot her engagement signs.

Once she's showing this relaxed interest in us, we make our first engagement with her. This is going to be in the form of verbal engagement, not eye contact. A soft, gentle voice is less threatening than eye contact. While we are reading our book, we're going to sense a moment when she seems reasonably relaxed, and we're going to say, softly and gently, 'hi Molly'. We knock a couple of treats her way.

Later, we repeat, adding a few more words. 'How are you?' followed by a couple of treats knocked in her direction. With further repetitions, we can get more verbose and relax the tone of our voice, talking more naturally and getting her used to our sounds. When she's comfortable with this, we start making brief eye contact. But we turn our attention back to our ever-so-thrilling book soon.

Gradually, gently, patiently and compassionately we step up the engagement. We start sitting closer to Molly; we speak and make eye contact more frequently. We reveal a treat on our palm-upwards hand, and see if she will come to take it from us. We don't thrust our hand toward her. Over time, she becomes more comfortable accepting us into her space and enjoys eating a few treats from our hand. We can start stroking her and showing more affection.

A slightly different method involves replacing the book with a dog toy, and playing with that as if it were the most absorbing form of entertainment we've ever experienced. This tends to work better with young dogs, or dogs who were at least once playful, and dogs who aren't so extremely anxious that the movement will frighten them. This might encourage such dogs to come toward us sooner and accept us into their space.

We have conditioned Molly to accept us using the treats and a highly non-confrontational approach. Now we are part of her previously very lonely comfort zone. It's us and Molly against the outside world. From this point, we want to attune Molly to the clicker and start doing some very basic training, all done within her comfort zone, so she gets the comfort and security of identifying us as leader. Then we can start on the journey of stretching her comfort zone in the same way we did with Alfred, using conditioning and operant conditioning with help from the clicker.

What can go wrong?

1. **Molly gets aggressive and snaps at us. Or she runs away from us.** We have simply pushed her too hard, and invaded

her space too forcefully. Or we have engaged with her, using (possibly accidental) eye contact too soon. If we take it slowly enough she should never feel the need to get aggressive.

2. **Molly seems to experience a relapse. She allowed us into her space, but a few days later starts showing signs of anxiety or aggression when we approach.** We need to be wary of entering her space too brusquely too soon. She is still feeling very delicate, so every time we approach we do so in a reassuringly non-confrontational way. We stop the approach if anxiety signs appear, but we don't leave (or we risk learned aggression). We drop some treats. We read our book again until she relaxes. We wait for her relaxed engagement signs – face relaxed, head cocked, watching us – and steadily continue the approach. Accepting us will likely have increased the radius of her comfort zone a bit, so we should be able to encourage her to approach us with some treats from a short distance away (just inside the utility room door, for example).

Summing up: Molly and Alfred

Most fear-induced anxiety sufferers will be in a state like Alfred (limited comfort zone where no anxiety warning signs appear) or Molly (no established comfort zone), so you should be able to use the above approaches to help your own dog.

Here are some of the key points:

o   For dogs like Molly, it is really important that they are the ones who choose their first place of security, which forms the heart of their comfort zone. Many fearful dogs show anxiety and aggression around the home because their owners, with all good intentions, have selected a 'secure' place for the dog. But it often won't suit the dog's individual preference and rather than feeling secure, his anxiety will be compounded when he is forced to endure it. Be prepared to put up with a bit of inconvenience. Some dogs will curl up behind the toilet or in your gym bag. Give your dog some alone time so he can find and settle in his space comfortably. This should be fine to do provided you have dog proofed the house, and shut off any areas which aren't safe. Go outside and do some gardening, don't spy on him. Once he's found a place to settle, start work on the 'Molly' approach.

o   We can see what a slow process is involved. Patience, compassion and perseverance will win through.

o   The clicker provides enormous assistance for both conditioning and operant conditioning once you've gone through the 'Molly' stage and reached the 'Albert' stage. It's a huge self detriment not to use one – but it also needs to be used properly, with secure attunement. Furthermore, a good grounding in simple commands is important for conditioning during the Albert stage. We want to give him simple commands, which we know he can complete successfully and easily. It is well worth spending lots of time reinforcing his ability to obey some simple commands while he is deep inside his comfort zone – using the clicker to help, of course.

o   Notice how, with both the Molly and Albert approaches, we never had to deal with the dog's aggression. It is the underlying anxiety we're working to address, and careful control means things should never escalate to the point where the dog feels he has to become aggressive. Keeping an eagle-eye out for the anxiety warning signs is really important for this level of control.

Other contexts

Once a good comfort zone is established and reinforced – the entire back garden, for example – we can start developing his comfort in other contexts. You might have a dog who is already happy at home, but gets anxious in other situations.

Your dog needs to be comfortable with the car, as this is going to be his initial comfort zone when he arrives in the new context (e.g., the park). If he is not yet happy with the car, refer to 'TRAVEL ANXIETY' (p203). Upon arrival, we simply use the same approach for Alfred above, working from his initial security of the car. You might have to do several trips before he is able to get out of the car without showing anxiety signs. During these trips, condition him by treating him in the car and asking him to do simple commands. Perhaps on the third or fourth trip, you'll be able to open the rear door of the car. But the dog will still stay inside. When he starts poking his head outside the door, sniffing the air, you'll know he is developing a relaxed interest. Use operant conditioning to reward this interest (click and treat it). When he eventually shows signs of wanting to jump out of the car, click and treat. With patience, and enough conditioning/operant conditioning, he should make his way out of the car by his own will.

Stretching his comfort zone in the park (or other context) works on the same principles as when you were doing it at home, but there are more unpredictable variables. A loose dog might run up to you, joggers might zip past, etc. There's not much we can do about this except ensuring everyone's safety by keeping the muzzle on, and making sure we model the confidence no matter what might come up.

Provided you are watching your dog's anxiety signs closely, you can start conditioning him to approach other dogs and people (using the Alfred approach). Enlist the help of friends or family members who have been fully briefed about your dog's fear-induced anxiety, and keep the muzzle on. It's going to take great time and patience, but there is no reason why you can't both succeed.

Secret Weapon No. 2

Let's give your dog a security blanket.

'Blanket' can be metaphorical; it could be a toy or item of clothing instead. But it's going to work much like a real security blanket for an infant. It is going to be something which your dog holds really strong positive associations with, so it gives him a nice sense of comfort whenever he sees it.

This won't work if you're still in the Molly stage with your dog, and you need to have some trust built up in your relationship. But if you've got an Alfred, whose comfort zone is very small, and you've done some training to build up a bond, it can be done and should help while you are stretching comfort zones.

Choose the object you are going to use for his security blanket. It helps if it's something he seems to like, but if he doesn't like anything then choose something that's safe for him to hold.

Give it a good rub up and down your body, in your armpits etc. This is best done after you've had a good workout so you're nice and sweaty. We want your scent all over it. If you've got a decent trusting relationship with your anxious dog, he'll like the smell of his 'blanket'.

Go to your dog when he's at ease in his comfort zone and show him his new 'blanket'. Whenever he shows interest in it – nudges it with his nose or sniffs at it – click and treat. See if he'll play with it a bit. Click and treat whenever he engages with it. Come back again later and do some more playing/clicking/treating.

Set up a little treasure hunt – bury the 'blanket' under some towels and see if he'll fish it out (this must be done within his comfort zone). Give plenty of clicks, treats and praise if he manages it. Find other ways to have fun with the blanket, and click and treat when he engages with it.

The aim is to build up a firm association, so when he sees the 'blanket' appearing he links it to comforting feelings of fun and the security of his owner's presence. To achieve the latter, we only want him to be with the blanket when you are around, so take it away when you finish each play session. You'll need to top up the scent frequently, too, so keep going out for those sweaty jogs and give it a good rub up and down afterwards.

With enough reinforcement of the blanket's positive associations, it can become really helpful when stretching comfort zones. When your dog's heeling, whip out his blanket and get his attention on it. You could let him carry it in his mouth if he wants. This should help distract him from anxiety. He'll draw on the blanket's positive associations and feel happier. Because your scent's all over it, it will help strengthen the dog/owner bond, and can be a useful aid for dogs who suffer from separation anxiety.

Secret Weapon No. 3

Our third secret weapon is a very powerful skill to train your dog to use. It can be hugely helpful when stretching a comfort zone. Secret weapon 3 is called 'touch it'.

The simple premise of this skill is that when you say the command 'touch it', your dog touches an object with his nose and receives a treat for doing so. The object can be anything you chose – your own hand works perfectly well, or a ball, or even a special 'target stick' which you can buy from pet shops.

This is effective because it works really well at distracting his attention from perceived threats. Imagine you are walking through the park and approach some playful dogs barking noisily. Your dog's warning signs appear at the edge of his comfort zone. You give the 'touch it' command and feed a treat when his nose bonks your hand. Give the command again, with another treat, and again. His attention is completely on targeting your hand with his nose, and he forgets about showing any anxiety toward the other dogs.

It does need to be used with some discretion – by simply distracting him from his anxiety, we are not necessarily helping him to actually overcome the anxiety. But with very anxious dogs who are quick to advance through the warning signs and get defensive at only slight provocation, 'touch it' can be really helpful for making positive headway.

It is easy to train, and even easier with a clicker. When your dog is relaxed at home, approach him with a treat curled in your hand. Let him get a sniff so he knows there's a treat in there, and wait for his nose to come into contact with your hand. (If you're using a different object, you'll need to coerce him to touch that instead.) As soon as his nose bonks your hand, praise him (click if using a clicker) and immediately let him have the treat in your hand. Repeat several times. He'll start to learn how to earn the treat, and will be keen to make contact with your hand. When you see him starting to grasp this understanding, add the command word 'touch it'.

METHODS: PACK AGGRESSION

Meet Conan: he's a canine tyrant who runs his pack with an iron paw. Want to sit on your favourite armchair? Too bad; Conan's on it. Want to get Conan out of bed and take him for a walk? Well too bad; Conan doesn't feel the same way. Want to leave the house and go to work? Too bad; Conan's taken up position on the doormat and there ain't no one brave enough to bust through that growling, teeth-baring monster. Samson, your cute little Pomeranian, just took a sniff at Conan's food bowl, and now Samson's got blood trickling out his ear. But Samson should know better: that's how things roll in Conan's pack.

Conan clearly needs bringing down a peg or two. But we need to remember: Conan's not really the overly domineering, cocky little blighter that he seems. What's going on in his mind? He feels the lack of a parent/leader figure in his society, and he (probably quite grudgingly) feels it necessary to fill that position himself. Poor Conan. He's had the burden of responsibility forced upon him because his owner has failed to assert a leadership role.

Pack aggression has close ties with leadership anxiety, and you'd do well to consult that section if you've got a Conan in your own pack. What Conan *really* needs is for his owner to step up and do a good job of being pack leader, which the 'LEADERSHIP ANXIETY' chapter is designed to help with. In this section, we'll explore some of the methods we can use to help Conan's pack aggression as it crops up in day-to-day scenarios.

Conan growls when I try to move him from the armchair

Here, pack aggression is compounded by learned aggression. All those times the owner has backed off when Conan starts growling from his comfy spot on the chair have taught the dog that his aggressive signs get him the outcome he desires. He's encouraged to use his aggression again, and he goes straight for it so there normally aren't any warning signs we can take advantage of. We need to reassert control.

The most effective and easy way to do this is, again, with the help of the clicker. Refer to 'THE CLICKER' (p234) if your Conan isn't yet au fait with the clicker; find the right time to attune him.

With the clicker ready, we're going to sit near Conan (in the second-best armchair) and wait for him to jump down of his own accord. Could take a while.

When Conan gets up, we're ready with the clicker. As he takes the jump down to the floor, we click and give a treat. We're using operant conditioning to reward Conan for his own action.

Now we wait to repeat. It doesn't matter if Conan's sitting in the same armchair or a different one: as soon as he makes the decision to jump off, we click and treat.

Conan's catching on – he's a bright spark, and he's getting the sense that if he gets down from this chair he's currently enjoying, he's going to get a treat. And lo and behold, it happens.

Conan's starting to get off armchairs more frequently. It feels good for us to be asserting some control over his behaviour, but there's no force involved here. It's entirely his choice, and he chooses the treat reward.

Once we've caught Conan's action of jumping off the chair several times, we can start adding a command word. We've got to watch him closely. When we see him about to make the decision to jump off the chair, we say 'off'. It's not a shout which might frighten him; it's just a calm instruction. Conan, once again, gets his click and treat.

We keep repeating, watching for Conan's moment of decision and saying the 'off' command at the right time. Soon he'll draw association between the 'off' command, the action he performs, and the reward he receives. We should now be able to ask him to get 'off' the chair when we want.

Several things are happening here:

- o Conan has learnt a new command.

- o Conan is submitting, in an entirely voluntary and amicable way, to the authority of his owner. He is getting a clearer understanding of who is boss, which is probably a great relief to him.

- o Conan is still allowed to enjoy his desired comfort, the armchair, but it is at his leader's discretion.

We can take further control over the chair by teaching Conan to get on it when we give permission, using a very similar approach. Start catching his decision to jump on the chair. Click and treat. Repeat. Add your chosen command word. Keep catching his decision, using the command word, until he builds firm association between the word, his action, and the reward. Use the command word alone to invite him onto the chair; click and treat his obedience. Click and treat; repeat and reinforce.

Now Conan will come and sit in front of the chair, look at you expectantly, and wait until you give the invitation to climb on it.

If all this sounds as if it might be a bit oppressive for Conan, it's really probably not. Most dogs love the security of having their owner clearly in charge. Furthermore, having recognised his owner's authority over the chair, Conan will more easily come to acknowledge the same authority in other contexts.

Conan growls when I try to get him out of bed

No one likes to be turfed out of bed, and perhaps the best way to approach this is to offer Conan something that really makes him want to get out of bed. So shake up his early-morning walk: start going to different places, give him more time off the lead, do some training on the walk so he looks forward to it more.

But we can condition his behaviour in this context too. We find a way to encourage him out of bed voluntarily. The best way to do this will depend on individual dogs. I find a good way is to pretend I've found something really interesting on the floor and make a big show of fiddling about with my fake 'treasure'. This might get Conan's interest piqued sufficiently to rouse himself out of bed; I click and treat immediately. Or we could drop a little 'breadcrumb' trail of treats for him to follow, clicking when he gets out of bed. Getting all excited with one of his toys, ready for early-morning playtime, might also work.

The crucial thing is that rather than forcefully approaching Conan and triggering his (learned) aggression, we're encouraging him to perform the desired action out of his own volition, which is key to operant conditioning. We can start adding a command word ('rise-and-shine!', maybe).

Conan won't let me leave the house

This is quite a clear example of pack anxiety. If a dog blocks his owner from leaving the house, that dog is feeling the responsibility of keeping the 'pack' together. He has assumed the leader/parent role which the owner should be fulfilling. Again, we need to assert ourselves back in the leadership position (see 'LEADERSHIP ANXIETY').

Conan's behaviour could also be prompted by separation anxiety. He has read the signs that his owner is about to leave, and associates this with the imminent onset of anxiety. So you will need to help your dog's separation anxiety if he is behaving like Conan, and work particularly on improving departure routines. See the relevant chapter.

We could use operant conditioning in this context. We might wait until he moves away from the door, and catch this with a click and treat until he learns the correct behaviour. Or we could teach him that he must always follow his owner through a door, and never go through it first (see DOORWAYS, p238). However, he will still be left suffering the same underlying anxiety. He wants to keep his pack together, and he doesn't want to be left alone. So the leadership and separation anxieties must both be addressed.

Another dog in the pack shows interest in Conan's food and gets bitten as a result

Dogs show aggression over food for two main reasons: 1) the dog has assumed a leadership position and is making a show of dominance (pack aggression); 2) the dog is anxious that his food is going to be taken away from him (resource guarding). In both cases the resulting aggression can be directed toward other dogs or humans who interfere with his food.

Knowing Conan as we do, this is more likely to be pack aggression than resource guarding. However, in both cases we're conditioning Conan to understand that it is okay for others (whether dog or human) to be around his food, the difference being that with pack aggression it's his self-assumed leadership position we're overcoming, whereas with resource guarding it's anxiety that needs to be addressed.

Because Conan, we suspect, is showing dominance over his food, we need to remind him that it is us, the owner and rightful leader/parent, who has true dominance. Sounds as if we're going to have to be very dominant, but we find comfortable, non-domineering ways to assert authority. Here are some ways to address Conan's food-related pack aggression:

1. We start hand-feeding Conan his food. This is a clear display that his food comes from the leader; it helps remove Conan's domineering sense of ownership over his food. This could diminish his inclination to make aggressive displays of dominance.

2. We make Conan work for his food. This might involve asking him to 'sit' before we offer the bowl, or perhaps asking for a (reasonably short) 'stay'. If the food comes as a reward from the owner for the dog's obedience, it helps to assert the pack hierarchy with owner as leader.

3. We find some food to share with Conan, but we eat first and him last. A banana works well if the dog likes it, or some cooked chicken slices (dogs can eat it raw; we shouldn't…). We let Conan observe us eating most of the chicken/banana, then we give him the last bit. This draws on his instinctive association of pack identity, in which the parent/leader eats first – so we can use this to assert our own position as leader.

4. We don't put his whole meal into the bowl, but split it into smaller spoonfuls. Each time Conan correctly obeys a command, ('sit', 'down', 'up', 'paw', etc.) he gets another spoonful dolloped into his bowl. Again, this reasserts our position as being dominant over food which he earns rather than owns.

5. Putting his food into different bowls each day, and giving it to him in different locations (just a different spot around the kitchen) may help to destabilise his identification of the food bowl as a familiar object which is 'his' possession that he can take ownership over. Methods such as this need to be used discerningly, however, as they can destabilise Conan's sense of steady routine and provoke more anxiety.

The above techniques should help diminish Conan's sense of ownership over his food, and lessen the chances that he will make aggressive displays of dominance. By asserting ourselves as leader/parent, particularly in the context of food, we have helped Conan understand that he doesn't have the right to discipline others in his pack over food-related affairs – that is the job of the leader.

Conan will need us to assert ourselves as parent/leader in other contexts too, so do consult the 'LEADERSHIP ANXIETY' chapter.

Pack aggression: summing up

We can see from the contexts we've looked at that pack aggression is generally resolved by reasserting ourselves as leader. We're not being punitive – we're not depriving the dog of the things he enjoys; Conan may still enjoy his armchair but he does so on our terms. This is widely benevolent for the dog's sense of security; he is being shown that he does not need to bear the burden of assuming the leadership position, as someone else (the owner) is capable of doing it for him.

Where pack-aggressive behaviour occurs elsewhere, it will normally be because we want the dog to do something he doesn't fancy doing, and he shows aggression because he feels more authoritative than the owner. We use operant conditioning to catch the behaviour we wanted the dog to do, using the clicker and treats to reward. We repeat, and associate the behaviour with a command word, so the dog starts performing the behaviour only when we give permission with the command.

METHODS: RESOURCE GUARDING

We tackle resource guarding differently to pack aggression because, although the two forms of aggression can look very similar, a dog who guards resources is suffering genuine anxiety that his food may be taken from him by another, whether animal or human. The pack-aggressive dog is merely making a show of dominance because his owner has allowed him to assume a leadership identity.

Aggression in resource guarding tends to manifest as a quick non-holding bite. This is actually a warning sign – the dog doesn't intend to do serious harm; he wants to warn the target away from his food (or other 'resource'). There can be other warning signs such as the dog hunkering down over his food as if protecting it, raised hair down the spine, and a general appearance of tension in the body. But the fast bite is common, so we need to be wary for it when we're around resource guarders.

Resource guarders may show aggression toward people as well as other dogs. In both situations, we need to alleviate anxiety by conditioning the dog to understand that it is okay for others to be near his food. Let's show him humans are safe first:

Guarding from humans

1. We wait for the safest possible resource-guarding situation to arise. This is likely to be when he is guarding something lower in value than his bowl of food – perhaps a chew toy, or old sock he's managed to get hold of. While this still isn't an entirely safe situation, his resource guarding may be slightly less virulent than when he's got a precious bowl of food.

2. We begin a good distance away from the dog, at a point where none of his resource-guarding anxiety is kicking in. This may be the other side of the room, or, for more committed resource guarders, the other side of another room.

3. We begin approaching the dog in the most non-confrontational way possible. This means no eye contact, and no looking directly at the dog. We don't make a direct beeline toward him; we try to make it look as if we're just wandering vaguely in his direction, by coincidence rather than by purpose. It might help if we're reading a book at the same time, or dusting the walls, or something which shows our main purpose is not to approach the dog.

4. We listen, and use our periphery vision, to check for the first sign of anxiety in our dog. He might pause in his eating/chewing, which shows he has tagged our presence and is anxious about it. Or his hair might raise down his spine. His ears might lower and tense. Ideally we want to spot something before it escalates into growling. When we spot it, we're going to toss a couple of treats toward him, hover in place for a moment, and then wander aimlessly away – we try to make it look as if we're not backing off; we don't want him to think any

aggressive sign on his part has achieved his desired outcome of making us go away.

5. Some really anxious resource guarders may be constantly displaying signs of anxiety when eating or playing with their toys — he might constantly be hunkered down over his object, hair always bristling. In such an instance, we try to get reasonably close before tossing the treats, but ideally not so close that his constant anxiety escalates into an aggressive sign.

6. Now we leave him be and wait for a similar situation to arise later, when we repeat the same process. Over the course of a few repetitions, we should find that we can start getting closer to the dog before his warning signs appear. This shows we are successfully conditioning him to think that a human's presence while he is eating/playing/chewing is not such a bad thing — it means he's going to get a few treats.

From here, you need to think about how you want things to progress. It's entirely possible that you could use the above conditioning process to shrink your dog's anxiety zone until you can come right up to his food bowl and pop those treats in it. You can practise the 'trade up' exercise, in which you swap his food bowl for something higher in value (a chunk of cooked chicken, for example), which, with practise, will allow you to safely take his food/toy/chew away from him. (This exercise is also best trained with a low-value resource first.)

But we need to think about whether this is really necessary or fair for the dog. In his world, it is completely natural — and appropriate — to warn pack mates away from his food if he's anxious about them taking it. Such anxiety-driven warnings do not mean he is a self-determined leader being overly dominant; any lower-down member of the pack will use these warnings.

This is where we see that rather uncomfortable dichotomy between the human and dog worlds. We can cheekily pinch a couple of chips from our partner's plate without hurting anyone's feelings, but dogs don't share the same playful attitude about their food/resources. I think, especially for anxious dogs, it is best to keep a respectful distance around his food once we have taken away the potential danger of a too-wide anxiety zone.

Nevertheless, there are a couple of ways we can take things further *without* aggravating our dogs' anxieties:

1. Hand feeding can be useful here, as it was with pack aggression. Feeding the resource guarder by hand is a generally safe way to establish physical proximity between the human and the eating dog. The idiom, he won't bite the hand that feeds him, might be trusted to an extent, but this exercise should still be practised with a muzzle. This gives further desensitisation of the dog's conviction that a human close to his food is a threat to his food.

2. We can teach the 'give' and 'leave it' commands (p233). The operant conditioning involved in training these commands is perfectly tolerable for anxious dogs, because it involves him being rewarded for his own decisions. Nothing is being forcefully coerced.

3. When it's meal time, we just put a small portion of the whole meal in the dog's bowl and give it to him. When he finishes, we add another portion, and so forth. This clearly gives the message that the owner's approach to the bowl is a good thing – it means more food.

Guarding from other dogs

Yogi and Daisy: two dogs who normally seem to be best friends. They go for walks together, play tug-of-war together, sleep huddled up together. But when they eat together, Daisy's anxiety kicks in and she sometimes lashes out at Yogi when she feels he's a threat to her resource.

We use a similar conditioning approach to help Daisy understand that another dog being nearby when she's eating (or enjoying any other resource) is a good thing.

We start this conditioning outside mealtime. After a walk, when both dogs have had lots of stimulation and have exorcised excess energy, is a good time. We bring Yogi and Daisy into the kitchen, where they normally have their meals, but remember we're not doing this at mealtime.

1. We're all going to share some treats. We give a couple to Daisy and then a couple to Yogi straight after. Daisy, the resource guarder, gets them first. Because Yogi gets his straight after we've given them to Daisy, she should be too busy with her treats to worry about snapping at Yogi. If she does snap at him, stop here. Try again later.

2. We keep giving treats, Daisy first, then Yogi, but we play with the rhythms a little bit. We start lengthening the gap between Daisy's treat and Yogi's treat. This helps Daisy see the turn-taking, sharing nature of the food-giving process – she sees, 'I get one, he gets one; I get one, he gets one'.

3. We need to further alter the rhythm so this becomes 'he gets one, I get one.' We give Daisy another treat, then Yogi. Pause. Now Yogi gets the next treat, followed by Daisy. Yogi, Daisy; Yogi, Daisy.

4. Later, we repeat the exercise, this time giving the first treat to Yogi (the non-resource-guarder), waiting a moment, then giving a treat to Daisy. With repetition, Daisy will be delighted every time she sees Yogi with a treat because it means she's going to get one too. It will help make her less protective and defensive over her food.

5. If Daisy is being too protective of her treats for this exercise to work, then both dogs will need to be trained to <u>sit</u> still while they are 'trading' treats.

6. When we're alone with Daisy in the kitchen, we get some treats ready (making sure she notices them and is in a state of anticipation) but we don't give her any yet. We wait for Yogi to show up (or call him into the kitchen) and then both Daisy and Yogi get some treats. This type of exercise helps condition Daisy to understand that Yogi is not a threat to her food – he is, in fact, the sign that she is going to get some food!

7. Now we can get to work during mealtime contexts. We can try handing out portions of meals, rather than the whole meal. A spoonful to Yogi, then a spoonful to Daisy. Another spoonful to Yogi; another to Daisy. This takes away Daisy's need to guard her food – it is no longer her possession which she needs to protect; it is something given to her at her leader's discretion. Furthermore, both dogs will be so focused on where the next spoonful is coming from that they will be distracted from their anxieties.

8. If Yogi doesn't mind being a bit of a 'lab rat' then we can try some operant conditioning exercises like this: while Daisy is eating, we bring Yogi (on the lead) toward her. We look for her first anxiety signs (hackles raised, whites of the eyes,

increased eating speed, etc.) and stop as soon as we spot them. We stay there with Yogi **until Daisy calms**, then we take Yogi away from the bowl. This teaches the resource guarder that her aggressive signals won't achieve her desired outcome (the other dog leaving), but her calm, non-aggressive attitude will.

Resource guarding can appear in a variety of contexts – the dog might guard a spot on the sofa, or another human being. We can still use the same conditioning process outlined above in these contexts.

However, we can't assume that a couple of conditioning sessions are going to make this sort of anxiety-fuelled aggression disappear forever – we have to be committed to reinforcing the conditioning fairly regularly.

When is resource guarding okay?

Most of the time, for most dogs. It's a natural, socially acceptable form of communication in Dog World. A little growl, or a white-eyed glare are normal signs of warning. In a food (or other resource) context, these signs do not indicate an leader-wannabe getting too domineering; any dog on the pack hierarchy will make them. They seem unacceptable to humans (growling at the dinner table doesn't normally constitute polite society) but that's the difference between our societies. It only becomes an issue if your safety, or the safety of another animal, is in question.

METHODS: TERRITORIAL AGGRESSION

Dogs are naturally protective of their territory. If his territorial protectiveness is becoming too aggressive and disruptive, we need to remind him that it's *our* territory, not his. Asserting our position as leader will help with this, so do consult the chapter 'LEADERSHIP ANXIETY' along with this section.

A couple of key points for working with territorial aggression:

o   This form of aggression can be particularly dangerous for innocuous visitors to our house. It's absolutely vital that we ensure anyone who needs to come to our front door will be safe from the dog.

o   Territorial aggression easily becomes learned, and dogs autonomously reinforce it for themselves. They take great pleasure out of barking wildly at their perceived threat, charging towards it, and feel very satisfied when they observe the threat fleeing from their territory. It's a nice exciting form of exercise for them, and they'll leap on every opportunity to repeat it. Therefore, we want to minimalise the potential for our dogs to autonomously practise it while we are helping them overcome this form of aggression. This may mean keeping them indoors and only letting them out into the garden under our supervision.

o   Territorial aggression is often worse in dogs who don't get a decent amount of exercise and stimulation; they're looking for somewhere to vent lots of pent up energy. Therefore, we need to ensure our dogs are getting plenty of good exercise on interesting, varied walks.

o   We won't achieve anything without a basic training and obedience programme going on. Get your dog clicker attuned and start regular training (p233).

Let's look at an example dog: Tyrone. When Tyrone first joined our home, he was pretty quiet. If someone walked past the front fence, he would often trot up to them and readily accept an affectionate greeting. After a few months, however, Tryone started to show signs of territorial aggression. The people who once stopped to give him a pat on the head now hurry past, with Tryone's vehement barking and slavering chops in pursuit. When we're indoors, any slight noise or disturbance from outside sends Tyrone dashing off to noisily carry out his protection duties.

In some respects, this is actually a good sign. It shows the rehomed Tyrone is coming to feel that our house and garden have become his home; his natural inclination is to protect it. However, in a human society, his behaviour is not acceptable so we need to condition it. His behaviour also indicates that he feels it is *his* territory to protect, rather than his owner's.

Assuming that we're also using the steps in 'LEADERSHIP ANXIETY' to assert that 'his' territory is actually his owner's territory, and therefore not Tyrone's job to protect, let's look at some practical steps to help overcome this territorial aggression.

Remember, we can't let Tyrone have free access to the outdoors while we're working on this. We keep him inside with us, and only let him out when we're supervising him.

Patrol duty

We're going to take Tyrone out on regular 'patrols'. These involve controlled walking around our territory, on the lead, using the 'heel' command (p238). At first, we may have to do just limited walks that stay close to the back door, but we want to get to the point where we can walk Tyrone everywhere throughout the territory without him becoming protective.

We get Tyrone into a heel, and walk him through some small circles around the garden. We keep clicking and treating his good heeling, being frequent with the clicks and treats to keep his attention on us rather than flitting to possible threats.

Any time he manages to keep his attention on us rather than getting distracted by something he might deem a threat or imposter – such as a bird landing on the lawn, or someone walking past outside, we click and give generous treats. We can use 'touch it' (p240) to help divert his attention from perceived intruders. If he does get distracted, and switches to protection mode (e.g. starts barking at the bird or passer-by), we simply take him back indoors and try again later (no physical punishment/verbal admonishment).

This exercise achieves several things. It helps Tyrone understand that we, the owner, are in control in our territory. He also sees that we are not threatened by things he might deem a threat, so it reduces his inclination to identify these triggers as threats. It also helps condition him to understand that he can only have access to the territory (garden) if he behaves in a non-protective way – as soon as he becomes protective, he is taken back indoors. The act of taking him back indoors is a form of punishment – we are taking away something he wants (access to the garden) so we need to be sensitive here. I like to do a couple of fun training exercises back indoors, with plenty of treat rewards, to continue to reinforce his good behaviour.

Keep repeating, extending the range of your patrol route. With enough reinforcement, we should be able to let Tyrone off the lead, but we'll keep him in heel while we're doing the patrol. With enough practice, he'll see the right way to behave outside and we should be able to start letting him out on his own – but we shouldn't do this until plenty of reinforcement with this technique and others has been achieved, to prevent relapse.

Operant conditioning

We can use operant condition to reconfigure the way Tyrone responds to perceived territorial threats. We do this indoors, because we can't have him charging outside and enjoying himself chasing off threats, as that will help his aggression become learned.

When Tyrone's in a reasonably relaxed frame of mind, we bring him into the living room and watch a bit of television or read a book. Tyrone can have a deer antler or other toy to keep him occupied. But we're going to keep a close eye on Tyrone, particularly when we hear a potential 'threat' from outside (someone walking past, dog barking in the distance, bird singing in a tree, etc.). We look for Tyrone's first warning sign (he stops chewing his toy/ears prick up/hackles raise) and we're going to immediately do what it takes to distract him.

For some dogs, we'll only need to call his name to distract him from the 'threat' and get his attention on us. Tyrone's a bit more committed to his protective duties, so we need to be more exciting. We jump up off the sofa, call his name, jump up and down a bit, then go and crouch in the corner of the room facing the wall. Tyrone's wondering what on earth's wrong with us and comes over to investigate; we click and treat generously. More anxiety-prone or stressed-out dogs might get upset by the energetic distraction we used, so judge it carefully for your own dog – it's got to be interesting enough to distract him from the threat, but not so wild that it compounds his anxiety.

It's crucial that we make the distraction at the earliest warning sign. We don't let the idea of a 'threat' get too established in his mind. With repetition of the above distraction exercise, Tyrone will start looking at us when he hears a 'threat' rather than immediately leaping up in a cloud of slobber and barks to dash out the back door.

With practice, our distraction won't have to be so dramatic and we can add a command word ('shh!').

Controlled explosion

Whereas the previous two exercises have been about focusing Tyrone's restraint, this one's more about letting him go all-out nuts in a (kind of) controlled way. It gives Tyrone stimulation and a way of venting his territorial energy in a way that is set on our terms. It is noisy, so not the best one if your prime concern is keeping life more peaceful for the neighbours.

When Tyrone's having a nice peaceful rest indoors, we go out into the garden, shutting the door, and we bring some balloons. The more the merrier. We inflate them, as quietly as possible so as not to disturb Tyrone's beauty sleep, and leave them lying around in the garden (grouped up or scattered; it doesn't matter). We go back indoors to the sleeping Tyrone.

We wake Tyrone with an exciting command word ('what's that!?') and keep using the command to encourage him out into the garden. If he's going nuts, that's fine – we go nuts with him. We let him find the balloons and do what he wants with them (pop them or just bark at them) repeating 'what's that?!' excitedly all the time. If he's popping the balloons, we make sure he's not eating any plastic.

During the balloon massacre and after, we click and treat generously, and keep repeating 'what's that?!'. If he gets distracted by a 'threat' (other than the balloons) we get him back indoors. Once the balloons are all dealt with (or once he's had enough time chasing/barking at them if he's not popping) we lead him back indoors.

With practice, we now have the 'what's that?!' command which allows Tyrone to go and have some noisy fun outside *at our discretion.* This can work really well in conjunction with 'shh!' above, as we now have full control over our Tyrone's energy. We can let him vent it when needed, but can keep him calm when we need him distracted from a territorial 'threat'.

Some dogs will be too freaked out or bored by balloons, in which case we find an alternative stimulus.

What else might help?

o   Determined practice of the 'stay' command (p237).

o   Taking back ownership of our doors by training our dogs to always go through a door after us, not before (p238).

o   We can invite someone over to our house (making sure we've briefed this person beforehand) to practise operant conditioning. Tyrone is indoors with us; we get him to 'sit' and 'stay', and click and treat his calm behaviour as the visitor approaches. If Tyrone starts getting aggressive (remember he is still indoors while the visitor is outside, so no one's safety is in question) we take Tyrone to the kitchen, and then go and greet the visitor (loudly enough so Tyrone knows the visitor hasn't gone away; we don't want his aggression to get his desired result or it will become learned).

o   Socialising Tyrone in controlled contexts such as obedience classes will generally lower his sensitivity to potential threats, as will exposing him carefully and gradually to new experiences (different walks, going to different places, etc.).

What not to do

Territorial aggression is one of the more enjoyable forms of aggression for your dog – it doesn't tend to spring from fear, it is just the dog enjoying one of his natural functions: to protect. However, we don't want to do anything that will teach him to associate 'threats' (the arrival of visitors, people passing by etc.) with feelings of anxiety, so we shouldn't contain him in a cage or crate.

LEARNED (AND GENETIC) AGGRESSION

Learned aggression is particularly dangerous and difficult to work with. Take for example a puppy who wasn't socialised well while he was growing up, and is consequently frightened of other dogs. When he is adopted from the rescue centre, he shows signs of anxiety when his new owner's other dogs are present, and starts snapping at them. They back off. He learns his aggression gets the desired result.

From now on, he doesn't bother with the warning signs because there is no longer any anxiety. He knows he can simply snap aggressively at any other dog he meets and it will go away. Some won't so he gets in fights.

We could use conditioning to teach the dog that other dogs are a 'good thing'; a very simple exercise would be clicking and treating when he notices another dog in the park, and increasing the clicks and treats as he comes closer.

But how can we do this safely? It is not possible. When we get close to other dogs, even if he has a muzzle he may still lash out aggressively. This will do nothing good for the other dog's anxiety, and injury may still occur through slashing paws. It is not fair to others to practise overcoming learned aggression in real-world contexts.

Therefore, the only safe and effective way to help, if you have identified a learned form of aggression with your dog, is through the help of professionals at dog obedience classes. They will be able to socialise your dog with others in a controlled setting.

In the safety of our home, we can look for triggers of our dogs' learned aggression and condition them with these. For example, he may suddenly leap at the front door when he hears a visitor approaching. This might look like territorial aggression, but the difference is there are no warning signs (no pricked ears, no hackles raised) – it goes from nothing to full on aggression in a single moment. So it is territorial aggression which has progressed to learned aggression.

We can use operant conditioning to praise the dog's calmness in the presence of such a trigger. We have to distract him from the trigger. When he's flailing at the door, we need to do whatever we can to get his attention away from it and onto us. This **cannot** be through force – the dog must make his own decision to shift the focus of his attention.

Call his name, use very high-value treats to tempt him away, make unusual noises such as calling his name in a sing-song voice or whistling, wave his favourite toy in the air, jump up and down a bit, run away into another room in the hope he'll follow, start making even louder noises and even more dramatic movements, etc. Note that those distractions increased in strength – we start small, hoping they will be enough to distract, before progressing to more dramatic ones. There is the risk that our more dramatic attempts to distract will only excite the dog's aggression further, so we have to hope smaller distractions will work. Significant trial and error will be required to find distractions that work for your dog without serving to increase his excitement.

As soon as the distraction succeeds, and his attention is on you – this may just be a pause in his barking and a glance in your direction – click and treat (enormously). During all this, the visitor must still be present outside (and the dog needs to know the visitor is present), so you'll need to enlist a volunteer who can keep making his presence known outside (without being too dramatic, or your distraction will never work). If the visitor leaves before you distract your dog, then the aggression has achieved its desired effect and the learned aggression is only reinforced further.

This sort of conditioning requires very firm reinforcement, so lots of practice is needed. It's tricky and often quite distressing to start with, but improvements can be seen reasonably soon. Your dog will start to get the point that stopping his aggressive behaviour gets a better outcome (the treat reward) than the one he would get if he persisted with his aggression. Really high-value treats help greatly.

The same sort of operant conditioning process can work for other forms of learned aggression. Our visitor above was safe on the other side of the front door. If your dog has a form of learned aggression that puts others in jeopardy, you cannot safely overcome it alone. Seek out one-to-one help with a professional.

AGGRESSION: FAQS

I don't understand – there's hardly anything in this chapter about dogs who are snarling and biting everything that moves, which is what my dog is doing. What am I supposed to do?

Because most forms of aggression are results of the underlying anxieties felt by the dog, we deal with those anxieties rather than the aggression itself. If things are under control when we're helping a dog overcome aggressive tendencies, the underlying anxiety should rarely escalate to the point where the dog becomes aggressive. Look out more closely for the pre-aggression warning signs, and condition your dog (as described in the methods above) to diminish these anxieties, and then he will be less likely to follow them up with aggression.

My dog has started becoming aggressive and I'm worried about the safety of my young children.

Children need to be educated to respect the dog's space, not to play with him too roughly, and to leave him alone when he wants to be alone. We can condition the dog using the clicker and treats to be more comfortable around children and minimise the risk of harm being done – but that risk is always going to be there. At what point can we start to trust a dog who once showed aggression toward children? Ultimately, considerable lifestyle adjustments need to be made in order to ensure everyone's safety.

I have recently adopted a puppy from a rescue shelter. She's lovely, and is doing well with learning basic commands, but I am worried about her early signs of aggression. She is very mouthy and sometimes bites.

Puppyhood is certainly the time to instil good behaviour. Put the focus on actively ignoring her mouthiness, and rewarding her appropriate behaviour. For example, if she tries to bite while you're playing with her, immediately ignore her by turning your back to her; don't say anything and don't look at her. Stay like that until she leaves you alone. This lets her know that inappropriate use of her mouth takes something fun (the game you were playing) away. Then get her attention on a toy; when she starts playing with that give lots of praise and a treat reward. She will learn which things are appropriate to put in her mouth, and which things are not.

When she's had her vaccinations, start taking her out to get her used to a wide range of different places and experiences. This will help her become more adaptable and tolerant as an adult, and will greatly help to lessen any anxiety-related aggression she might otherwise suffer.

I don't know what to do about my French bulldog. He is seven years old, and lives with our English bulldog who is two. They normally get on fine, but when my husband and I are relaxing on the sofa in the evening he (the Frenchie) starts getting aggressive with our English bulldog. It doesn't matter who our French bulldog is laying with; he'll start looking at our other dog, ears back, hard stare, growling, etc. Our English bulldog puts up with it for a bit, but starts to growl in response after a while. I eventually put the French bulldog in the kennel to keep everyone safe, because I don't know what else to do!

This is a clear example of resource guarding. You, or your husband, or the spot on the sofa is the 'resource' which the French bulldog is guarding from the English. Unfortunately, by taking the French Bulldog away and shutting him in the kennel, you're validating his anxiety. He's worried that the English is going to take his 'resource' from him, which does indeed turn out to be the case when he's taken off to the kennel. You're right, of course, to ensure safety — but perhaps consider a muzzle instead while you are working on overcoming the resource guarding.

We need the French Bulldog to see the presence of the other dog as a good thing, rather than a threat. Consult the conditioning methods in the 'resource guarding' section above.

My eleven-month old dog escaped from the garden recently. He chased a small child and bit her on the heel. When I walked him the other day, he jumped at an old lady. We saw someone else with three dogs, and he was fine with them. If I go jogging with him, he'll nip at my ankles.

This confident, boisterous puppy is growing into a dog who thinks he is in charge. This is essentially leadership anxiety - he needs help to understand that he is not the boss, and can't bully others around. He was probably fine with the other dogs because one of them asserted a leader position over him.

I just got a dog from the rescue centre who is fine with people but shows anxiety and gets aggressive around other dogs, especially big dogs.

This is likely fear-induced anxiety. Keep him muzzled, and look for his earliest anxiety warning signs when you approach other dogs. When you spot them, condition him using the method described in the fear-induced anxiety section.

A reminder:

Training is absolutely vital for overcoming aggression. We can use training, such as simple 'sit' and 'heel' commands, to put dogs at ease when they are on the edge of their comfort zones and start showing anxiety signs. Many owners who feel they are not making any progress overcoming their dog's aggression are not committed enough to regular training. We've just got to grab that clicker and get on with it.

.

Separation anxiety

Your dog is a social animal. You are a central part of his society. He is inherently inclined to feel anxious and stressed when he is separated from his society's members. It is unusual for a dog *not* to suffer from separation anxiety if his owner has to leave him.

When one goes about the process of finding a puppy/rescue dog/etc. to join the home, there is a barrage of advice along the lines of 'you shouldn't get a dog if you will have to leave it alone for more than an hour or two'. Unfortunately, with the pressures of modern life, and the need to have a full-time job in order to afford those luxuries such as food and a place to live, this sort of ideology would leave dog ownership to the privileged few. Many wonderful dog owners who have to work to make a living would miss out on their dog-owning vocation – and many dogs would miss out on having a wonderful owner. We should resist the urge to feel guilty for leaving our dogs alone; modern life very often makes it an inevitability.

However, there are limits to what is safe and healthy for a dog. The amount of alone-time which is tolerable will depend wildly upon the breed and individual character, but no dog should be pushed too far. While employed in a full-time job, I would never leave my dog alone for the full working day. If I were not able to get home during lunch to take him for a sprightly walk, I would get a dog walker to do it or put him in day care.

For the intervening hours of aloneness, there are many things we can do to alleviate our dogs' loneliness and anxiety. Most dogs respond well to at least some of these methods; it is unusual to come across a dog whose separation anxiety can not be diminished at all.

Let's first take a closer look at some of the symptoms, as it's not always obvious when a dog is suffering from separation anxiety.

DOES MY DOG HAVE SEPARATION ANXIETY?

Separation anxiety causes dogs to become stressed when they are left alone, so we want to look for signs of that stress occurring. An obvious sign is that your dog is all hyped up when you return home and gives you an overly-enthusiastic greeting – however, some dogs will just be pleased to see you, so his hyperactive greeting doesn't necessarily mean he was stressed in your absence.

If he seems exhausted (lots of panting; quite quickly flops down on the floor after he's finished greeting you), this indicates that he has been expending a lot of energy by getting stressed when you were away. This will be corroborated if he's drunk a lot of water. Any signs of pacing up and down also indicate he has been in a state of nervous restlessness.

Destructive behaviour can be a sign of separation anxiety, depending on what he has been attacking. Items with your scent on them will be a first target – he can smell you on them, and might chew or scratch them up in his attempts to search for you. If your dog associates your departure with a particular doorway or window (for example, he's often seen you leave through the front door before your long absence or can watch you get in your car from the living room window) he might scratch and bite in these areas in an attempt to escape and follow you.

He might spend time howling or barking in distress during your absence – neighbours will report this to you, or you'll hear it when you pull up outside and get out of your car. Weeing and pooing indoors is also a sign of stress – dogs do not naturally like to go to the loo in the space they consider to be their 'den' – or incontinence.

Destructive behaviour alone is not a reliable marker of separation anxiety – it could also be a result of boredom, leading to depression, rather than anxiety.

WHAT NOT TO DO FOR A DOG WITH SEPARATION ANXIETY

There's a fairly popular perception that dogs who have a tight bond with their owner are more likely to suffer from separation anxiety, and therefore it is best not to let your dog get too clingy and dependent on you when you're with him at home.

This is not the right approach. A dog who has a good relationship with his owner is confident in his owner, and is more likely to trust that his owner has not abandoned him. Furthermore, altering your behaviour with your dog (e.g. creating more distance between the two of you at home in an attempt to alleviate his separation anxiety) will only serve to destabilise his confidence and exacerbate anxiety.

Getting a second dog is sometimes touted as the magical panacea of separation anxiety. Whilst many dogs will be happier with the company of a canine comrade, the pair of them are still going to be without their master so you could end up with two dogs suffering the same anxiety.

Anti-bark collars are quite popular with people whose dogs suffer from separation anxiety. Barking, and the consequential complaints from neighbours, are understandably a big concern and something we want to stop. Shock collars may be effective at silencing the barking, but they are compounding the underlying stress suffered by your dog. To help his separation anxiety, we need to help him forge a sense of confidence and ease when he is alone. Zapping him is not going to help him feel confident. He becomes quiet because he is a nervous wreck and dreading the next electric shock. If we work on easing the underlying anxiety, he won't feel the need to bark because he will start to feel happier when he's by himself. Additionally, we can use training methods to practise stopping barking through his own volition, rather than through the threat of being electrocuted.

FUNDAMENTAL ESSENTIALS FOR HELPING A SEPARATION-ANXIETY SUFFERER

We'll begin with some of the basic, and fairly obvious, ways to help:

- o   Ensure your dog has his basic needs met during your absence. Separation anxiety causes stress, which means he will be drinking more water than usual, so make sure he has access to plenty.

o Exercise is crucial. Take him for a good, energetic walk before you have to leave. Let him expend his energy outdoors, so he's less likely to expend it nervously pacing up and down your living room. A dog who hasn't been adequately exercised will be overly stimulated when you leave him, and will be anxious to find ways to vent this stimulation – which will compound the anxiety he feels at being left alone. Very often, separation anxiety can be significantly alleviated by giving your dog a thorough work out in the morning. It may mean you have to get out of bed at an ungodly hour, but your dog will appreciate it.

o Make sure you have fully dog-proofed all the space your dog will have access to when he is alone. No wires in chewing distance, no breakable or chewable objects within reach, etc. Bear in mind he will be hunting hard for objects to amuse himself with, so be extra vigilant when dog proofing.

Those are the very basic essentials. We'll look at further approaches below.

MONITORING THE SITUATION

One tricky aspect of treating separation anxiety is that it's rather difficult to monitor progress – because you're not there. When you are trying out new methods and approaches, you need to be able to see if they are helping your dog's anxieties or not.

Fortunately, with today's technology, the ability to monitor your dog throughout the day is surprisingly accessible. If you have a smartphone or tablet with a camera on it, you can download an app which will enable you to turn it into a remote CCTV camera

– for free. You can then set up your phone/tablet in a place where it will have good coverage of your dog while you are out. By logging in to the app from another computer (e.g. your desktop at work) you can access a live feed of your dog. If you don't have access to a computer at work, you can simply download the camera feed when you get home. The app highlights periods of movement so you can skip to these rather than watching the entire thing. This allows you to see how effectively the new strategies are helping. The name of the app I have used is 'Manything'.

SEPARATION IN PUPPYHOOD

Ideally, we want to prepare our dogs for the experience of separation when they are still a puppy. It's said that puppies are highly adaptable and tolerable to new situations until they are 14-16 weeks old, after which point they can become uncomfortable with unfamiliar changes to their routine. So the window from 12-14 weeks gives us a great opportunity for him to have a little practice at being alone; then he'll be better prepared for the real thing.

Don't panic if your dog is older – it doesn't mean he is beyond help. But you can skip this section and go onto the next.

When your puppy is at least 10 weeks old, and he feels comfortable and familiar with his space at home (which has been rigorously puppy proofed), you should start trying to leave him alone for short amounts of time. At first, this will just be leaving him shut indoors while you spend a short time in your garden. You might step this up to a 10-minute stroll to the shop. Then make it a bit longer until you get to the point where you're leaving your puppy for an hour or so. Remember he has limited bladder tolerance at this age, and he needs to have frequent toilet trips until he is a year old, when he should be able to comfortably hold his bladder for a few hours.

Due to your puppy's very poor short-term memory, there isn't much difference between being alone for 10 minutes and being alone for an hour. However, it is best to start with very short times in case he gets upset or gets himself into some sort of mischief.

This is a good time to start desensitising your puppy to signs which might trigger separation anxiety. Think of the signs he might come to recognise as indicators of your departure – fetching your briefcase, opening car doors, etc. Introduce these signs. Go out to the car, start the engine, then return to your dog. This sort of exercise will diminish the potential for these signs to become triggers of separation anxiety.

You will need to set up a place indoors where your puppy knows it is okay to go to the toilet in an emergency. This should be as far away from his sleeping/playing/feeding and drinking place as possible. Some newspaper is fine, or you can get cheap strips of artificial plastic grass from big garden centres. Although your puppy is unlikely to be convinced that this is real grass, it gives him a very distinctive texture that makes it easy for him to distinguish between toilet space and non-toilet space. Teach him it is okay to wee and poo on his newspaper/fake grass by leading him to it when he shows signs of needing the loo, and rewarding him generously when he does his business on it.

Because your puppy is still young, he tolerates unfamiliar experiences well. Your absence won't be such a shock to him as it would be to an older dog who is not used to being left alone. Simply giving him this practice at an early stage will likely foreclose the possibility of serious short-term separation anxiety occurring as he grows older.

PREPARING SPACE

Setting up a nice comfortable space for your dog, whether he's young or old, requires some careful consideration and tailoring for his individual preferences. Does he prefer to have some space to roam around in, or does he feel more secure in a smaller, more confined space? Monitor your dog to see what would be most comfortable for him.

One thing to definitely avoid is setting up a separate space that your dog only goes to when you leave him – for example a utility room or spare bedroom. Every time you put your dog here, he will know you are going to leave and his anxiety will be immediately triggered. It is best to designate a space that your dog normally has access to and uses routinely throughout the day; this space should include the place where his bed belongs. You can close off access to other parts of your house where it might not be safe for him to go. Install a baby gate at the bottom of the stairs – they are cheap and most don't need to be drilled into the walls.

Find some things that have your scent on them and leave them accessible to your dog in his living space. Some pre-laundered socks, your pillowcase, or a towel, for example. Having your scent close by may prove to be comforting for your dog – on the other hand, he might think he can find you by following the scent, which can cause greater stress. If you come back to find your pillowcase and socks shredded, this tactic may be causing more stress than comfort.

Don't forget to ensure your dog's space is at the right temperature for his breed and preference. If he's under stress, his body temperature will be higher than normal. Use air conditioning and buy some fans if necessary to keep the space cool enough.

THE DEN

It is important your dog has a place he considers to be his 'den' – that is, a place where he feels comfortable and secure. This becomes particularly important for separation anxiety sufferers – if he doesn't have such a place of security within access, his anxiety will be compounded.

The place where you happen to flop down his bed may not be the same place he decides to designate as his den. If you notice he tends toward a particular spot when he wants to rest – perhaps it's a cosy niche under the stairs, or behind your sofa, or under the dining-room table – that's the spot he has chosen for his den, and it ought to be made accessible to him when you are out.

However, not all dogs are naturally inclined to find such den-like areas. Dogs are often considered to be den animals, but this isn't entirely accurate. A den animal is one who digs a burrow into the ground and spends his rest time in it. This would include animals such as foxes, rabbits, badgers, etc. You don't see many domestic dogs doing this; neither does the dog's ancestor, the wolf.

What wolves and dogs are inherently ingrained to use are 'maternal dens'. A pregnant dog/wolf will feel the urge to scratch out a very sheltered, protected den where she can give birth to her puppies, who will spend the first couple of months of their lives in this den. This leads to the natural association for the dog of a den-like place being one of safety, security and comfort.

But once grown up, the dog becomes an open-air beast. For example, adult wolves will sleep out in the open, where they have good access to and visibility of the land around them. They may seek to establish a den-like space when feeling ill, or when pregnant, but will otherwise prefer the open.

Therefore, we can see that not all dogs will want to spend time tucked up in a secure 'den' while you are out of the house. If you've got a dog who likes to get up on the windowsill so he can observe the outside world, this may be where he will be most comfortable resting. We should never forcefully confine our dogs in a small space such as a crate – even den animals have the freedom to come and go.

Many dogs will enjoy having a den because it draws on inherent associations with the maternal den and provides a feeling of comfort and security, though the extent of this association will depend on the breed, individual, and nature of whelping.

An appropriately sized crate can be a good way to provide such a den-like place for your dog. Remember the door should not be shut, and the crate should be in a place that your dog has chosen as his secure spot, rather than one his owner's chosen for convenience. See the 'CRATE TRAINING' section (p242) for more detail on how to set up a good crate, and how to help your dog get comfortable with it.

THE TOILET

A puppy of three months should be able to hold his bladder comfortably for two hours; this time increases by one hour for each month of age. Adult dogs should never be expected to hold their bladder for more than eight hours – which is too long for any dog to be comfortably alone.

Most adult dogs who have had at least some semblance of house training will prefer to postpone their toilet trips until you get home and they can get out into the garden; nevertheless, it is a good idea to set up a toilet space where he knows it is fine to go to the loo should the urgent need arise.

If your dog has a den space, the toilet should be as far from it as possible. Lay down some newspaper and if your dog has a wee on it while you are around immediately give him a generous treat. He'll come to understand that it's fine to go to the loo on this spot.

You can buy fancy indoor dog toilets, or you can set up some artificial (plastic) grass, available from big garden centres, with newspaper beneath. This gives an easily distinguishable texture which will help your dog differentiate between toilet spots and non-toilet spots.

Never get upset with your dog if you come home and find he's had a wee or poo somewhere you don't want him to. Thanks to his short-term memory, he won't have a clue what you're so angry about, and his stress levels will rise.

DEPARTURE AND RETURN

Key moments to focus on when helping alleviate your dog's separation anxiety are when you leave the house, and when you return. Dogs become adept at recognising the signs that mark your imminent departure – getting your coat, car keys, etc., and these signs will trigger his anxiety. He will become stressed even before he is left alone, and this keeps his anxiety perpetuated after your departure. We want to teach him to disassociate the signs of your departure with his feelings of stress. This will allow him to be in a calm mood when you depart, and will allow him to maintain more easily the restful, peaceful state we want him to enjoy while we're away.

First, you need to identify the signs which your dog associates with your imminent departure. There are probably lots. They can include:

- o Verbal language you use with your dog. 'Good-bye', 'be a good boy', 'see you later', etc.

o   Specific actions such as getting up off the sofa after watching the morning news, or washing up your breakfast.

o   Heading toward a specific door – if you always leave through the front door, your dog will recognise this.

o   Pre-departure actions such as putting on your coat or fetching a briefcase.

o   Even your general mood – if you exhibit nervousness, reluctance, haste, etc. before you leave your dog will detect this and come to recognise it as a sign.

The above are just some of the things which your dog will come to associate as stress-inducing signs of your departure, but there are many other possibilities. Turning off the television or switching off lights may also become signs for your dog.

We can give immediate benefit by changing our pre-departure routine as dramatically as possible. Leave your coat in the car so you don't have to put it on when your dog is present, leave the house through a different door, put your keys in a different place, do something different to what you normally do immediately before you leave. This will disrupt the language your dog has been reading – he won't see the same signs which previously triggered his stress, and will likely help him maintain a slightly calmer mood as you depart.

Of course, it's going to be difficult for you to find a different departure routine every day. There are only so many different doors you can leave from, and only so many places where you can stash your coat and car keys. So we also want to start working on diminishing the negative association our dog holds toward the departure routine.

To do this, we practise fake departures. When you've got a day off work, and you're relaxing in front of the television with your dog, start launching into the departure routine. Run through the familiar signs such as switching off the television, fetching your coat, keys, etc. Don't worry if your dog starts getting anxious, because you're not going to leave the house. In fact, when you see him start to get nervous, that's a good point to stop the pretence. Put your coat and keys back down, go back with him to watch TV on the sofa together. Or, even better, take him outside for some fun play time in the garden. Do a training session with him. Have a tug-of-war with his favourite toy.

By practising that sort of pretend departure, but ending it on a very positive note, you will help him reconfigure the associations he holds with your particular departure signs. It is ideal to practise it at the normal time of your departure, but on a day when you don't actually have to leave him (so eight o'clock on a Sunday morning, for example) but it is good to practise it at other times during the day, too.

Remember, dogs form strong associations, so it's going to take time and perseverance to see beneficial effects with this approach. But it's worth sticking with.

Shaping a positive departure routine

Once you've worked on the above disassociation method, helping your dog become less stressed by your departure signs, you should start shaping a routine which will help your dog see your departure as something positive, enjoyable, even something to look forward to.

The most important part of this routine will be the exercise that comes before it. Make sure your dog has had a generous walk in the morning, with plenty of time off the leash. This will leave him in an endorphin-fuelled good mood, and will mean he has much less pent-up energy to expend during your absence.

After his walk, give him his breakfast. If your current meal plan doesn't involve a breakfast, you might consider restructuring it. Dogs are naturally inclined to rest after a good meal in order to ease digestion, so this may well help him get into a restful mood. Of course, you need to factor in your dog's bladder/bowel functions – if he likes to have a poo an hour or so after a meal, this won't be the best course of action. Most adult dogs, however, will be happy to hold on until they are let out at lunchtime.

After breakfast, you've got some nice time when he can settle down calmly while you do the things you need. Have your own breakfast, gather your bits for work, get a shower, etc. While you're doing this, your dog should be nice and calmly settled. Many anxious dogs need training to help them do this, so refer to 'SETTLE' (p239) in the 'Training' section.

Now you're going to get ready to leave. Get your coat, keys, pop your briefcase down outside the door. But before you finally leave, you're going to have a final bit of fun in the garden doing something your dog enjoys. Kick a ball around with him, play fetch, or do a few training exercises with some nice treat rewards. Apart from letting your dog expend a bit more energy to facilitate his rest, this also allows him to build association between your departure signs and something fun.

You're probably a bit late for work now, so it's time to take him back indoors. You need to have his entertainments ready (see the next section, 'OCCUPY HIS MIND'). Put these down for him so he immediately has something really enjoyable to keep him happy. His attention must be on one of these entertainments, and not on you. If this is proving difficult, you need to step up the quality of the entertainments you are providing. You also need to make yourself virtually invisible. As soon as the entertainments are in place, quietly leave. Say nothing, do nothing apart from quietly closing the door behind you. Any affectionate last goodbye is just going to serve as another sign to trigger his anxiety. It is therefore important that you are ready for work *before* your final playtime in the garden, and your briefcase/bag is outside the door so it can be picked up discreetly.

Departure: summing up

So, let's run through what a complete morning/departure routine should look like:

1. Wake up early and take your dog for an energetic walk. Most dogs will want forty-five minutes to an hour, depending on how much of this can be off the lead.

2. After the walk, give him some breakfast.

3. Now he has some settling time, with our help training him to do this at first (see 'SETTLE', p239. While he's settled, you go about your necessary affairs.

4. Get all your departure bits together, coat on, briefcase/bag outside the door.

5. Take him out into the garden for final playtime, making sure it's fun and positive for him.

6. Bring him indoors and give him his entertainments (see next section). Once he's occupied, and his attention is on the entertainment rather than on you, quietly leave with no final goodbye ceremony.

The return

Returning home to a separation-anxiety suffering dog can be, as you'll know, an extremely frantic affair. There he is, scrabbling at the door while you unlock it, whining and crying away, then he's leaping all over you in paroxysms of ecstasy because, finally, you're with him again.

Unfortunately, if we respond to his very enthusiastic, anxiety-driven affection with our own affection, we're teaching him 'learned anxiety'. We're showing him that his stressed-out response is going to get him what he wants, so he'll only feel encouraged to get into the same sort of nervous wreck next time we come home. Instead, we want to teach him that being calm is the right thing to do.

It seems harsh, and can often be very difficult, but we must ignore our dogs while they are greeting us with anxiety-fuelled enthusiasm. No matter how much he leaps up at you, how much he whines and cries, just completely blank him. Don't look at him. Don't speak to him. Even if he gets a bit rough, don't admonish. Just go indoors and go about your business – take your coat off, get yourself a drink, etc. – but in your periphery vision watch for the moment when he calms. He will look away from you and will stop hungering for your attention. Now you can greet him – not too rambunctiously, keep it calm but affectionate. Take him outside for a bit of gentle playtime if he can manage this without getting too crazy.

Ideally, we wait for this moment of calm to come spontaneously from the dog. However, particularly stressed dogs may need training to help them calm. If he's showing no sign of calming after you return (you might need to be patient, so give him time to calm of his own will) then ask him to sit. You could use 'settle' training to help him calm. Then you can greet him.

OCCUPY THE MIND

We've looked at departure and return routines – but what about the intervening hours of loneliness your dog must endure?

If he has had sufficient exercise and stimulation during his morning walk and pre-departure playtime, then he will find it easier to spend some of your absence resting. Because you have worked on setting up a den-like place – whether this is a crate or bed in his chosen area, or a place where he can observe his surroundings – he will have somewhere to go where rest comes more easily.

But we want to provide plenty of stimulation for when he isn't resting. When he's up and about during your absence, we want him to have a good range of things which will focus his mind, keeping it distracted from his anxiety.

The extent to which his separation anxiety is successfully alleviated can depend quite heavily on the quality of these stimulants, or 'entertainments', you provide, so it is worth investing time to find the best things for your dog's particular preferences. If you manage to find things he really enjoys, he will start to look forward to his alone time.

Here are some of the best entertainments I have discovered:

Stuffed KONG

KONGs are sturdy rubber toys available from pet shops and online. They are hollow, meaning you can fill them with a stuffing of your choosing. Get the right size for your dog – it shouldn't be so small that he might be tempted to chomp the whole thing down, and not too big so he is completely stuffing himself with the treats inside. KONGs are strong, good quality toys and very difficult for most dogs to destroy. Extra-tough versions are available for determined chewers.

I like to fill my KONGs with some small bits of lightly cooked chicken, a little bit of cheese, a bit of white bread, some yoghurt (fat-free Greek or natural goats' yoghurt are best), perhaps some pureed pumpkin, and maybe a bit of peanut butter.

Stuff the KONG the night before your departure with your chosen ingredients, and put it in the freezer. Most dogs love the frozen texture, and it keeps them busier for much longer.

A stuffed KONG works brilliantly as the first entertainment – when you put his entertainments down after final playtime, the KONG will likely be the one he will go to and get to work on while you discreetly leave. His mind will be so focused on the frozen stuffing that he won't notice you leave, and his mind will stay focused on it for a decent amount of time.

If you find he's showing little interest on the KONG, or not enough interest to keep him distracted from your departure, you may need to try different ingredients. Or perhaps an alternative entertainment will work better.

Treasure hunt

This is a marvellous entertainment which involves leaving small treats hidden around the space your dog has access to during your absence. Similar to the KONG, you'll need to find treats your dog enjoys. There's no need to use a large quantity of treats – it is the action of hunting them down which keeps him occupied and happy, rather than the actual eating.

Take three or four of your chosen treats and wrap each up in a piece of old newspaper (this preparation is good to do during your dog's 'settle' time, pre-departure). After final playtime, when you're laying down his entertainments, hide these treat-enclosing pieces of paper in different spots around your dog's space. He needs to be distracted by another entertainment (e.g. the KONG) while you do this.

Make the hiding spots obvious at first – you can increase difficulty once he's got the hang of the exercise.

Once he's finished with the KONG (or other entertainment) he will want to go on a hunt, sniffing out each treat. The paper they are wrapped in adds an additional layer of stimulation; he'll be entertained trying to work the treats out of the paper.

It's a good, stimulating entertainment because it works his prey drive and requires firm mental focus to track the treats down. Energy is being expended, facilitating rest.

You'll want to make sure he's not actually eating the newspaper. Although doing so isn't likely to damage him, it's not something we want him to do habitually. Therefore, this treasure-hunting entertainment is a good one to practise when you are around at first. If he eats the newspaper, try a different wrapper such as old socks, or just hide the treats under some towels, inside shoes, etc.

KONG Wobbler

Another KONG product, the Wobbler is a fantastically stimulating entertainment. It's a large, strong plastic, self-righting toy with a hole in the side. You put some treats or dry dog food inside. Your dog has to knock the Wobbler about with enough energy so the food comes out of the hole.

This is another entertainment which stimulates his prey drive, and demands high mental focus – so it's a great distractor from anxiety. You could put some of your dog's kibble in it, so he gets a bit of brunch/lunch, or just a few high-value treats. A lot of these entertainments revolve around treats, so don't fill it with too much to prevent him getting fat.

One disadvantage of the Wobbler is that it can be knocked about quite violently by big and enthusiastic dogs, which may do a bit of damage to the paint at the bottom of your walls.

Interactive toys

If you've got the cash to splash, you can buy some terrific interactive toys to help keep your dog distracted from anxiety. These again revolve around dispensing treats, so be careful not to fill them too much.

The 'memory trainer' is a fantastic toy, though quite pricey. It consists of a unit which you put the treats into, and a separate unit with a button on it. Your dog's task is to press the button, which releases treats from the unit (it works via wireless remote control).

Some training is required to teach dogs how to use it, but this can be a lot of fun and most dogs get to grips with it easily. Once he's got the idea of how it works, you can increase challenge and stimulation by moving the button further away from the unit, and even hiding it around your dog's space.

The memory trainer can be purchased for about £40/$55 if you dig around online.

Another great interactive toy is the 'Foobler'. This is a treat dispensing ball which your dog has to knock about in order to get treats out. However, the Foobler comes with an extra twist in the form of a programmable timer. You can set this to release treats at varying intervals, e.g. one hour, into the internal holder, at which point they can be released onto the floor when your dog knocks the Foobler about. Each time more treats are released, a bell rings – you can teach your dog that this bell means he should go back and play with his Foobler, because he'll get more treats.

A huge advantage of the Foobler, is that it gives a prolonged entertainment. Your dog can play with it, get the available treats, then an hour later more treats will become available so he can have more fun with it.

There are plenty of other interactive toys available, though some of them can be a bit fragile. The memory trainer and the Foobler are my dogs' favourites – and they have proven to be reliably strong.

Homemade interactive toys

It's very easy to knock up some stimulating toys to keep your dog focused and distracted from anxiety.

Simply take an empty plastic milk bottle and toss one or two treats into it. Getting them out will be quite a mental conundrum for your dog, and could keep him engaged for a long time. Try it when you're present first, so you can check he doesn't try to eat the plastic.

Add challenge by making a hole in each side of the plastic milk bottle, about one third of the way down from the top. Thread a length of string through the holes, and find somewhere to tie each end of the string; it should be quite taut so the bottle hangs upright above the ground. Before you leave in the morning, stick a couple of treats in the bottle so your dog can enjoy his new airborne interactive toy.

The long cardboard tubes from kitchen-paper rolls are great to use for disposable toys. Put a couple of treats into the middle of the tube, then keep them in the middle by stuffing a couple of rolled-up-paper balls down the tube on each side of the treats. Your dog will be able to smell the treats, but has to figure out how to get past the paper in order to reach them.

Old cereal boxes, or any other type of cardboard box, are also really good – toss a couple of treats inside and close the box; let your dog go to town on it. Wrap newspaper around the treats first for extra challenge.

Any sort of toy you can make which offers the dog some sort of challenge before he can get to the treat is the sort of thing he needs to keep his mind working when he's not resting. Just be sure to test your toys out while you are around your dog, so you can make sure he's not going to eat something he shouldn't.

Non-treat entertainments

Treat toys work well for dogs who are motivated by food, but we don't want our dogs to be stuffing too many unhealthy treats down their throats.

You'll want to find your dog some good chew toys that he enjoys exercising his jaws on. Chewing releases endorphins, and helps him feel at ease. Unfortunately, it can take quite a bit of trial and error to find something your dog enjoys. Not all dogs are switched on by straightforward Nylabones.

A chew toy that most dogs really enjoy is a deer antler. These are available in all shapes and sizes from pet shops. They are hard wearing, and last a long time, but are safe and natural chews for your dog. You can store them in the freezer to keep them fresh, and dogs seem to really like the sensation of a cold deer antler in their mouths.

You can buy some quite interesting chew toys from pet shops – there are special ones which have a crunchy, intriguing texture when chewed.

Something as simple as a carrot, stored in the freezer over night, can be a really fascinating chew toy for dogs. Or you could take an old hand towel, soak it in water, and freeze it. Many dogs will really enjoy the refreshing, satisfying chewing experience this provides (at the cost of a wet mess on your floor).

Try dropping some ice cubes in a bowl before you leave in the morning. Dogs love ice cubes, and they can be stimulating to chase around in the bowl.

Many dogs love chewing sticks, which aren't safe because of splinters – but you can buy specially treated 'chewing wood' from pet shops or online which your dog might really enjoy.

Rotating entertainments

Don't give your dog the same entertainments each day. Change it up so he keeps getting something different every day. You might have one or two as regular daily staples, such as the stuffed KONG, but the others should be kept varied.

Typically, on one day I will give my dog a stuffed KONG in the morning, along with a treasure hunt and a deer antler from the freezer. When I come home for his lunch break, I will give him a Wobbler to keep him amused for the two hours I am away in the afternoon.

The next day I will again give the KONG in the morning along with the memory trainer and a milk bottle or cardboard tube toy. In the afternoon, I will wrap up a duck foot (my dogs have raw food) in paper, and put it in a cardboard box.

Dogs who suffer more intensely from separation anxiety may need a greater amount of daily entertainments than the above examples. Keep monitoring him while you are away, using your smartphone or tablet if possible, and make sure he is really enjoying the entertainments you leave him with. If they are not distracting him from his anxiety, you will need to find alternatives (or treats which he considers to be higher in value).

SOUND THERAPY

Some owners of separation-anxiety suffering dogs like to leave music or a radio/television playing while they are away, believing it helps soothe their dogs' anxiety. Others condemn such an approach, believing this noise is simply going to frighten the dog and add to his distress.

I believe background sound can do a lot to alleviate separation anxiety, but it must be used in the right way.

A radio is a perfectly good source for background noise – doesn't matter whether you use a musical station or a talking one, but keep it consistent. Radios have the added bonus of being portable, so you can move one into your dog's space easily. Television is also fine, though this is going to have a larger impact on your energy bill. You can also use your computer to access channels on YouTube which provide special music that is supposed to be relaxing for a dog to listen to.

It really doesn't matter what source of background noise you use, provided it is not a noise or volume which is going to upset your dog.

What you mustn't do is only play your chosen background noise when you leave the house. In this case, it just becomes another sign which he associates with the anxiety of being left alone. Whenever the radio starts playing, it will immediately awaken his anxiety.

Instead, decide what background noise you are going to use and start playing it in the evenings when you are around your dog. Make a special point of turning it on when you have playtime with your dog. Play it when you're training 'settle'. Make sure he starts to associate it with being in a good mood – when he hears the sound, he knows he's in for a good time.

Don't change the variety of background noise once you have done some work building up these positive associations. If you've been using a classical-music station, stick to it. Same if you've been using a talking station. My dogs are avid listeners of BBC Radio 4.

With enough positive exposure to the noise, the positive associations will help keep your dog in a relaxed frame of mind. Turn it on when you return from your morning walk, so it's playing during his settling time. Don't turn it on immediately before you leave.

GIVE THE DOG A PHONE

You can use your home telephone to give further environmental reassurance in a similar way to 'sound therapy' described above.

Start building your dog's positive association with the sound of the home phone ringing. Do this simply at first; call your home phone with your mobile, and when the phone starts to ring (and your dog hears the ring) give a couple of treats. Repeat a few times. He'll start to get positive vibes whenever he hears the phone ringing. If your dog naturally gets tensed up when the phone rings, you'll need to do quite a bit of reinforcement of this step over several sessions and days.

Then, along with the treats, give your dog a burst of playtime when the phone rings so he enjoys himself even more. Start practising 'settle' with the phone ringing. With enough work, he'll build up firm association between the sound of the ringing phone and the enjoyable, relaxing sensation he experiences with the treats, playtime and settling.

Now, go outside into your garden or take a quick stroll to the shop, leaving your dog alone indoors. After about ten minutes, give your home phone a ring. If you've done enough reinforcement of the previous steps, this should encourage your dog to feel happy and relaxed. Shortly after the phone stops ringing, go back indoors. Follow the standard 'return' protocol (don't respond to your dog in any way, even avoiding eye contact, until he is calmed). Later on, repeat the same process. Keep practising it daily. Your dog will start to associate the sound of the phone with your arrival, which could help him feel comfortable.

When you're practising, put some treats nearby the phone and help him find them when it rings. You could then wrap a treat in newspaper and leave it behind/nearby the phone for him to find when you call while you're away from home.

Some dogs, however, will just get hyped up in anticipation, so monitor his reaction to the phone call and don't continue if he is getting too stressed. Just work on associating it with the happiness of playtime and 'settle'.

If your dog responds well to the phone call, then keep building association between it and your arrival. Next time you have to leave him for an extended period, give him a call just before you return. Start calling him earlier, leaving a longer delay between the call and your return home.

If he responds well, the sound of the phone ringing and all the positive associations your dog now holds with it will help ease his mood no matter what time of day you call him. For this to be really effective, it relies on your dog establishing strong positive associations so go back to reinforcing those using treats, playtime and 'settle' if it doesn't seem to be working.

CLEAR LEADERSHIP

Up to this point we have largely been working with environmental aspects of your dog's separation anxiety. We have ensured he has a place he has chosen himself as being one that provides a sense of security, we have populated his space with stimulating activities that distract him from anxiety, we use sound therapy to draw on his positive associations and help him maintain a calm state, and we are following the correct departure and return procedures to help him keep control over a calm state of mind. We also ensure he receives a good amount of exercise and stimulation before we leave him.

However, there is more to separation anxiety than environmental factors, and we can not rely on those alone to fully alleviate his issues. How secure the dog feels in the absence of the owner is influenced quite significantly by the nature of the relationship he has with his owner.

It is a common misconception that the dogs who have the closest, tightest, strongest relationship with their owners are the ones most susceptible to separation anxiety. Some owners feel this to be true because they observe that their dog is very 'clingy', always following them around and wanting to share their company all the time. Because the dog has such a close relationship with them, they think separation anxiety is caused when dog and owner are apart.

In fact, dogs who are 'clingy' with their owners tend to be ones who are not entirely confident about the relationship. Or, more accurately, they do not have a good sense of pack identity. Every dog's pack needs to have a clearly established leader, or parent, for its members to feel secure. Dogs need to know who is in charge, who to take leadership from. If they don't have a clear idea of who belongs in the parental position, they feel insecure. This is when 'clingy' behaviour might be observed. The dog becomes clingy because he is feeling a lack of guidance, leadership, or authority in his pack identity which makes him nervous and unable to relax. He might be following the owner because he's looking for leadership, or he might be feeling pressured to assume the leader position himself. Some behaviour that is mistaken for being 'clingy' can actually be the dog's attempts to assume a parent/leader position – for example, when he climbs onto the owner's sofa and manoeuvres himself into the position the owner was formerly enjoying. This isn't because the dog is overly dominant, it is because he feels his pack lacks a parent/leader and feels pressured to (probably reluctantly) assume the position himself. Conversely, a dog with a good understanding of who holds the parent position can enjoy the confidence of knowing that someone else is definitely in charge; he can relax comfortably and independently, not feeling he has to follow his owner about in search of a sense of security.

When out on a walk, some dogs will go roaming off by themselves. Others will cling closely to their owners, even when off the lead. Many people would consider the latter dog to possess a more secure relationship with his owner, but this is not the case. The dog who goes roaming off is confident in his owner's position as parent/leader. He trusts the leader will be there when he returns, and feels secure to wander off on his own for a bit. The latter, clingy sort of dog most likely does not have the same confidence. He is always wondering, who is the leader? Am I the leader? Should I be in charge? And he clings closely because he can't resolve this identity crisis.

Therefore, these sort of identity issues can contribute greatly to a dog's separation anxiety. If he has a clear idea of who adopts the parent/leader position in the pack (and this should, of course, be the owner) then he will feel more secure in the leader's absence – this is because dogs are inherently inclined to understand that the leader does not desert the pack. In a way, the dog feels similar anxieties to the owner when they are both apart. An owner who understands and trusts his dog won't have to spend every moment of the day worrying that his dog is shredding the carpet or scratching out escape passages through the back door. And a dog who understands and trusts his owner's position as parent/leader won't have to spend all his time worrying that the owner has deserted the pack.

If our dogs are clingy, it doesn't mean we're bad owners, or we've done anything wrong. Different dogs perceive their pack identities differently, and some just need more reinforcement of who adopts the leader position.

This means we can help our dogs' separation anxiety greatly by working on our own authority as pack leader. Reinforce for your dog, using the right methods, that you are the parent/leader and he will feel more secure and at ease.

Consult the following section called 'LEADERSHIP ANXIETY' for guidance on how to help your dog establish a healthy appreciation of your leadership role using the right (positive) methods.

BEREAVED AND REHOMED DOGS

A couple of months ago, one of our dogs passed away. Since then, our other dog has been getting really distressed when he's left by himself. He wees indoors, which he never used to do, and he's destroying things in the house. When I'm at home he's really clingy, following me about and looking for me whenever I go out of sight. His separation anxiety is just getting worse and worse. I don't know how to help.

This sort of scenario is really common and very upsetting. Two dogs who coped quite happily when left alone, but when one sadly died the other began suffering terrible separation anxiety which nothing could seem to fix. However, if you've read the previous section ('CLEAR LEADERSHIP') you won't find it hard to understand what's going on with this bereaved dog.

The loss of his companion has resulted in a pack-identity crisis. It is very likely that the other dog filled a leadership position in the pack; with his passing the remaining dog now lacks a clear understanding of who the parent/leader is. What seems like separation anxiety is actually leadership anxiety. Rehomed dogs can suffer a similar crisis – they are torn from their familiar pack (even if this was just himself and owner) and now they are not sure who the leader is. We address his separation/leadership anxiety by reasserting our role as parent/leader in the pack; continue to the next section for help with how to do this.

.

LEADERSHIP ANXIETY

IS MY DOG A WOLF?

This question rears its head a lot in the dog-training world.

While I'm writing this, there sits in the corner of my living room a great lump of dog; he's watching me, a string of dribble hanging from his mouth, tongue lolling, quietly panting in anticipation because he knows it's nearly time to go and play football in the garden. He's the sort of dog who sits placidly while small children queue up to give him a hug. He's got more in common with a beanbag than he has with a wolf.

And yet, he likes to walk around in circles a couple of times before laying down, which is what his lupine ancestors did to flatten the grass for a comfier bed. He likes to sleep outside the back door, where he can observe his surroundings, just like his great great great great grandfather, the wolf. If such behaviours remain inherent, how much of a stretch can it be to imagine that the dog seeks the same hierarchical pack structure as the wolf? And as we all know, this is a structure which requires the dominant supervision of an 'alpha': the leader.

Or is it? The concept of 'alpha' animals leading the hierarchy of wolves' social structure was first developed by a zoologist called Roland Schenkel (p246), who studied captive wolves in Basel, Switzerland, in 1947. Schenkel observed in his studies how a single dog-and-bitch pair of wolves 'carry through their rank order as single individuals of the society; they form a pair...By control and repression of all types of competition, both of these "alpha animals" defend their social position'. It's from this pioneering study that our concept of the 'alpha wolf', who ambitiously climbs the social hierarchy, was born

Schenkel also makes several parallels in his paper between the wolf and the domestic dog, drawing the conclusion that if wolves structure their hierarchy under an 'alpha' position, this must be the same for their relative, the dog.

However, more recent findings – this time based on studies of wolves in the wild, rather than in captivity, have brought into question this traditional understanding of the 'alpha'-oriented hierarchy. Zoologists such as Lucyan David Mech and M.W Fox (p246) came to the conclusion that there is in fact no such thing as a dominant wolf who seeks to fight off competition and become the 'alpha' leader of the pack. The social structure, they found, is in fact much more similar to humans' own; what Schenkel had taken to be 'alpha' wolves were really much closer to simply being parents. There is, according to Fox and Mech, no inherent sense of rank among wolves; offspring simply look to their parents for leadership in the same way as many other species do – including our own.

Many dog trainers and behaviourists keenly debunk as a myth the notion of 'alpha' leadership, but most of those trainers will agree that dogs do, nevertheless, require a source of leadership that would come from a natural 'parent' figure.

So what does this mean for the modern dog owner? It would seem that what our dogs need is not for us to be a dominating 'alpha' leader of the pack; rather, we should model our leadership on the way a parent would lead a child: compassionate discipline, with plenty of love and affection.

Throughout this book I refer to the need for the owner to establish a 'parent/leader' position in the 'pack' – and what this literally means is establishing a 'parent'-like role. In response to the question, we can draw the rather endearing conclusion that no, your dog is not a wolf – he's more like a child, and he needs the same sort of leadership from us as children need from their parents.

LEADERSHIP ANXIETY: A DEFINITION

'Leadership anxiety' can be roughly defined as the lack of confidence a dog feels in his owner's fulfilment of the parent/leader role. This lack of confidence triggers anxiety in various situations, and may result in aggression if the dog feels a need to fulfil the missing parent/leader role himself.

LEADERSHIP ANXIETY IN CONTEXT

Let's look at an example situation to see how leadership anxiety manifests in the real world.

The owner is walking his dog, Colin, out in the forest. They turn a corner to find a couple of horses (with riders) ambling toward them on the path. Colin hasn't seen many horses before, but fortunately his owner has him on the lead.

The owner is worried that Colin might start barking at, or otherwise get excited about, the horses, so pulls him off the path and tells him to 'sit'. Colin obeys, but keeps his eyes fixed on the horses. The owner keeps reminding him to 'stay', but as the horses approach, Colin jumps up and barks at them. The owner, embarrassed and apologetic, has to cling on to the lead while the horses make their way past Colin's snapping chops.

What's really going on here? Did the owner do anything wrong? Absolutely not. Colin might have detected some anxiety from the owner, particularly when he was dragged off the path, but the owner was doing his best to keep Colin's attention off the horses. Although nothing massively incorrect was done by the owner, the above situation speaks of a general lack of confidence the dog feels in his owner's position of parent/leader. Colin wasn't able to trust his owner was in control when the 'threat' of the horses approached, because he doesn't have enough general confidence in his owner's leadership. Therefore, Colin feels the pressure to deal with the situation himself.

Overcoming this kind of leadership anxiety is all about building more trust and confidence in the relationship. Even dogs who have wonderful relationships with their owners, full of reciprocal love and affection, can (very often) lack the kind of confidence which the dog needs to feel comfortable in stressful situations like the one faced by Colin.

Leadership anxiety has a compounding influence on many other forms of anxiety, especially fear-induced anxiety, territorial anxiety and separation anxiety, so it's crucial to work on this to help your dog's general wellbeing.

LEADERSHIP ANXIETY: WHAT NOT TO DO

If we keep in mind our need to provide a parent-like figure for our child-like dog, we start to see a reasonably clear model of the type of leadership to provide. Let's consider a couple of the 'old ways' for asserting leadership:

- The 'alpha roll' – the owner forcibly rolls the dog onto his back and pins him there, making firm eye contact, holding him in place until he submits to the superior strength of his owner.

- Using shock collars to punish misbehaviour and to condition the dog.

- Not letting the dog lay on the bed, sofa, or anywhere he might feel his status is equal to the owner's.

- Restricting the amount of love and affection the owner shows to the dog.

- Standing in the dog's bed to remind him it belongs to the owner.

- Taking away toys from the dog during playtime, and taking food away during mealtime, again to make the dog understand that food and toys belong not to him, but to the owner.

- Using physical punishment to condition the dog's behaviour.

Would we do these things to our children? Not if we want to avoid calls from social services. So we shouldn't do them to our dogs, either. These old methods (some of which are still practised today) are based on intimidation, forced submission, and a misconception of the 'alpha'-oriented hierarchy. Some of them might indeed keep the dog's behaviour in check, but at the cost of plunging him into a world where he is frightened of everything – including his owner.

Modelling our leadership on a 'parent-child' basis sounds lovely, but there are complications to consider – mainly in the form of communication. When the child has stolen money from your wallet to buy some cigarettes, we can use clear communication to explain why we're not giving him any pocket money for a month, or not letting him out to play with his friends tonight. Our clear explanation allows the child to know why he is being punished.

When our dog has had a wee on the carpet, and we come home three hours later, we can't use the same language to explain why the dog is being punished – and he will have no idea why he is being punished. He won't remember weeing on the carpet, and he certainly won't interpret the received punishment as a consequence of his weeing.

Sometimes punishment (never physical, never frightening) can have a place when asserting our leadership over our dogs, and we'll look at this later, but we have to be extremely careful when using it. Unlike in the human parent-child relationship, the dog won't be able to understand, in the majority of cases, why he is being punished.

DOES MY DOG HAVE LEADERSHIP ANXIETY?

More than likely, yes. It's more unusual to come across a dog who shows no trace of leadership anxiety whatsoever than those who have it to some extent. If your dog shows signs of leadership anxiety, it doesn't mean you're a bad owner; it doesn't mean you haven't shown your dog love and affection; it doesn't mean you've done anything wrong. It's hard to establish a secure bond of trust and confidence with an animal – much harder than with a human child, I would argue.

The marker of a dog suffering from leadership anxiety is that he exerts his own will in a situation that he finds stressful – rather than listening to, and obeying, his owner's will. Dog's with a mild degree of leadership anxiety (the normal, common amount) will therefore be difficult to control in unusual situations (such as Colin with the horses). Dogs with more prominent leadership anxiety will be difficult to control most of the time, and are more likely to escalate into aggressive behaviour.

I see top-level obedience and agility dogs, who compete in competitions, that still exhibit leadership anxiety when situations become a bit stressful. I also see dogs who are habitually disobedient much to their owners' bemusement, the reason being that they just need a firmer idea of who their 'parents' are.

OVERCOMING LEADERSHIP ANXIETY: KEY ELEMENTS

Many behaviourists talk about the importance of 'consistency' when working on a strong owner-dog relationship. This refers to consistency in attitude – never getting frustrated and remaining positive toward your dog; consistency in rules – if you don't let your dog on the sofa, make sure everyone in the house adheres to this; consistency with praise and rewards – if your dog obeys a command don't neglect the treat, and so on.

This sort of consistency is important for allowing our dogs to get a clear understanding of what is expected of him, but there are wider implications for the dog-owner relationship. We have to remember the unusual nature of dogs' memories. They have very weak short-term memories, but very strong associative memories. The treat you gave to him for being a good boy ten minutes ago is entirely forgotten – but if you've been *consistent*, he will come to associate you as someone who offers nice treats when he obeys you.

Every encounter and interaction we have with our dogs develops their associative understanding (and memory) of who we are. The more consistent – and fair – we make our approach during these interactions, the more trust and confidence they will come to feel toward us.

This goes a long way to explaining why **regular training** is so important for developing a trusting relationship. Training builds up a wonderful associative understanding in our dogs. He gets used to the feeling of doing what his 'parent' tells him to – not because he is forced or frightened into doing so, but because he knows he will be rewarded. The consistency makes him feel confident that he will be rewarded; he starts to enjoy being led by his parent and trusts in his parent's authority and treat offerings.

Dogs whose training stops after they are taught to wee outside rather than in the house, and maybe trained to obey simple 'sit' and 'down' commands, in puppyhood lose out on developing these wonderfully healthy associations in their parent. It doesn't mean the relationship is any less loving, but it does mean that he doesn't associate his owner as being an authoritative and reliable parent as much as a dog who gets to enjoy regular training.

Therefore, a regular training programme is the absolutely vital, fundamental building block for overcoming leadership anxiety.

Exuding confidence and calm authority is also vital. As the parents, we need to be consistently calm and confident – particularly when we expose our dogs to potentially stressful situations. I once worked with a gentleman who couldn't understand why his three little Norfolk Terriers got so excitably vocal whenever a visitor arrived at the house. But the reason soon became clear one morning when the postman arrived. The owner immediately got himself into a panicked frenzy, because he was anticipating his dogs' bad behaviour. He went outside flailing his arms around with a tone of despair in his voice as he desperately tried to herd his flock of terriers back indoors. His dogs were picking up on his very tangible anxiety, and this not only compounded their own anxiety but also showed them he was not in authoritative control of the situation, so they had to step up and take charge in their own noisy way.

Developing the confidence-based relationship by exposing yourself and your dog to new experiences is also really powerful in overcoming leadership anxiety. If your dog has the confidence to obey you in your back garden, that's great - but it's not going to fly when you get out into the stresses of real-world situations. We need to keep sharing new experiences with our dogs – explore new walks, meet different people and different dogs so their confidence in us is cemented in a variety of contexts.

TRAINING THE RIGHT WAY

When training, we want our dogs to build up associations of confidence and positivity. So, we keep training sessions short (five to ten minutes) and fun (plenty of rewards). We make sure to finish them with something we know the dog can do (such as a 'sit') so they always end on a positive note.

It helps enormously to use a clicker, as this helps to give crystal clear positive feedback for when the dog has done something we're pleased with. Simply spending the first couple of sessions attuning your dog to the clicker, and reinforcing his understanding of his name, will be a really positive way to start (see 'TRAINING', p233).

Try to make your short daily training sessions as routine as possible – at roughly the same time each day is best.

Not all dogs are particularly motivated by treat rewards, so find something else he really likes. Some dogs like nothing more than having a tennis ball tossed to them for a quick playtime after they'd done something really well.

Obedience classes are hugely valuable for building your confidence-based relationship with your dog. Apart from giving a professionally guided boost to your training, they also help your dog associate you as a competent leader outside the sheltered context of your house and garden.

Finally, training isn't about turning your dog into a perfectly subservient robot (unless you want it to be). Think of it as a way for you and your dog to bond together, sharing a fun, productive and mutually satisfying task that helps build your confidence in one another.

PUNISHMENT

As compassionately authoritative 'parents' to our dogs, we will on occasion need to show that we are displeased with their behaviour. When your dog's getting over excited and jumping all over your back, you can't very well nod approvingly and utter 'good boy, good boy'.

But we know that physical punishment is very destructive to building a healthy and trusting relationship – so what can we do?

Well, we can employ a technique known as 'negative punishment', which is pretty much the polar opposite to 'positive reinforcement'. When we click and treat a good behaviour, such as a successfully completed 'sit' or 'stay' request, we positively reinforce the dog so he feels encouraged to repeat the behaviour.

He wants to do the same thing because he expects the reward. With negative punishment, we deprive him of his expected reward when his behaviour is inappropriate.

For example, when he's jumping all over your back he's expecting to get your attention. We deprive him of this 'reward' simply by completely ignoring him. We become boring, immobile, silent statues, not responding to him in any way until he calms down. Then we give him a big fuss, to show it's his self-control that gets him what he wants (our attention).

If he's a manic whirlwind of barking when you get home from work, you blank him until he calms down. Go and watch the television, or make your cup of tea – don't acknowledge his existence until he calms. This negative punishment shows him that his behaviour won't get him what he wants. When he does finally calm down, we switch to positive-reinforcement mode by giving him a big fuss as a reward. This sort of negative punishment is the only form of punishment I advocate using.

APPROACHES AND TECHNIQUES FOR BEING A GOOD 'PARENT'

Let's look at some specific strategies we can use, aside from your regular training programme, to help our dogs build confidence in our parental leadership.

Overcome a fear together

Lots of people are frightened of housework, and lots of dogs are frightened of vacuum cleaners – what better way to bond than to overcome this mutual fear together?

If your dog flees for safety when the vacuum cleaner comes out of its cupboard, then you can develop his confidence in you by teaching him that the hoover is a nice thing to be around, rather than something to fear.

Have the hoover on the floor, not switched on. Coerce your dog toward it by calling his name and using treats. Click and treat when you can see he's overcoming his anxiety to get closer to the vacuum cleaner. Keep encouraging him to come closer, rewarding every step. Put a couple of treats on top of the diabolical machine so he's encouraged to get even closer. Don't push too hard too soon – it might take a few sessions before he can actually approach the vacuum cleaner and start sniffing around it. Just keep rewarding him, with the help of the clicker, when he summons the courage to get closer.

When he seems comfortable to get close, try turning the hoover on (not when your dog is standing next to it). Then repeat the above process with the machine running. He'll come to associate it with the very pleasant experience of getting lots of rewards, and his previous fears should become largely forgotten. Furthermore, he's developed confidence in you because you've shown him not to be frightened of it.

A note of warning: you might find your dog gets a bit too keen on your vacuum cleaner, and hoovering sessions become more cooperative than is practical!

See the 'TRIGGERED ANXIETY' section (p215) for more guidance on how to overcome your dog's very specific fears of other trigger objects.

No free lunch

Get into the habit of making your dog 'earn' all the food and treats that come his way – for example, asking him to 'sit' before he gets his bowl of food.

This may sound like a rather authoritarian method, but it helps to instil the understanding in your dog that you are the 'parent' who provides the food, and develops his overall feelings of security and confidence in you as leader.

The physical examination

Work on giving your dog a good, thorough, physical check-up. This involves examination all his various bodily regions for injuries and general condition. For a good check-up we should be able to look inside the dog's mouth to check for gum health and any dental issues; we should be able to lift up his paws and check his pads for condition; we should be able to get a good look down his ears; we should be able to lift up his tail and have a look at what's going on under there, and we should be able to run our hands over all parts of his body to check for any hot spots or sensitive patches that might indicate injury.

Practising this is not only going to be really appreciated by your vet, who'll suddenly find check-ups much more manageable, but will also help to build that bond of trust between you and your dog. Not many are initially comfortable with being probed by their owners, so it'll take a bit of work.

Start simply by stroking your dog when he's nice and calm, giving him a few treats to reward his calm response to your touch. Slowly, gradually, start moving your focus to more sensitive areas. Lift his ear flap (or stroke raised ears) and again reward his calmness. Gradually move to other parts of his body – try lifting up his paws or lips. Keep practising over several sessions, working up the intimacy, and using plenty of treats to reward his placid response to your physical examination.

Grooming

Similar to the physical check-up, grooming can help develop a trusting bond. It relies on quite intimate physical contact which many dogs are initially uncomfortable with, but they'll start to enjoy it once they begin to feel more secure.

Make sure you choose the right grooming implements for your dog's coat. Slicker brushes are quite nice for shorter-haired dogs with non-matted coats; pin brushes are good for longer coats. Make sure whatever you use isn't going to tug and cause the dog physical distress; you could use a de-tangle spray to make it a bit more comfortable (so long as your dog isn't going to be put on edge by having it sprayed on him).

Start by getting your dog settled and calm, then run the brush down his back very gently. Give him a couple of treats to reward his calm response. Stick with this for the first few sessions; just run the brush lightly over a non-sensitive part of his body, rewarding his calmness. If he gets uncomfortable and wants to leave, let him – just try again a few hours later.

He'll soon start to enjoy the feeling of the brush on him, because he'll associate it with receiving a reward. You can now start working on other areas of his body. Try the legs and chest. Keep up the rewards.

Both the physical check-up and grooming require a degree of submission on his part, by allowing you access to the vulnerable areas of his body. When you can do it comfortably, it shows that you're building up a really good, trusting, confident relationship. Work on them slowly, and keep the rewards coming.

The power walk

The daily dog walk provides a great opportunity for the owner to establish parental authority in a fun way – but it might require a bit of adjustment to your usual routine. Quite often, walks become something in which the dog takes charge. He sets the pace, he decides when to stop (to sniff an interesting bush/lamppost), sometimes he even sets the direction while the accompanying owner ambles along obediently, caught up in a daydream and little more than a passenger on the dog's expedition.

While there's nothing wrong with this – both dog and owner are enjoying their walk – it doesn't much help to establish the owner as the parental authority. For this, the owner needs to become a much less passive part of the walk. Behold 'the power walk':

The first step of powerwalking is to have your dog on a lead. Even if you walk through land where it is safe for your dog to roam freely, stick him on the lead for the power walk. It's essential that you have control over your dog.

Now, set off at a brisk walking pace with your dog at 'heel' (p238) – even a gentle jog if you/your dog are fit enough for it. Just make sure you're going faster than your normal dog-walking pace. This will take your dog by surprise because it breaks the routine – but he'll probably enjoy the excitement of it.

Shake up the power walk by changing pace unpredictably – suddenly slow down the initial brisk speed and insist your dog heels with you very slowly for a bit. Then speed it up again.

Keep making things unpredictable by making sudden changes of direction. You can even turn right around and walk back in the direction you've just come from for a bit – then turn around again and continue your walk. Make sure it's always you who is determining speed and direction. If your dog wants to stop to sniff something, don't let him.

This is a really clear and effective way of showing your dog who the leader is. However, it's also really good fun for him. Most dogs love the unpredictable excitement of the power walk – with practice, they start to enjoy (and feel comfortable) allowing the owner to take leadership over the walk.

Powerwalking needn't dominate your entire dog walk – it can just occupy 5-15 minutes of it, and the rest can be spent at a more relaxing perambulatory pace. Combine it with some 'heel' training – when your dog gets good at 'heel', he can lose the lead and still keep up with your pace/direction changes.

Take some treats with you for the power walk; offer some up during the exercise to reward his obedience and to keep things fun.

Hand feeding

Meal times are often when dogs are at their most obedient – they are quite happy to satisfy the owner's demand for a 'sit' if it means getting their teeth around some good grub sooner. But this obedience also stems from the clear indication provided at meal times that the owner is the leader/parent figure – just like children look to their parents for food, the dog recognises that the provider of food is the parent/leader figure.

We can strengthen this recognition by making the feeding process a more 'hands-on' affair – simply feed your dog out of your hand rather than out of a bowl. (Obviously, this can get a bit messy if your dog is on a wet or raw diet rather than dry.) This gives the dog a much more potent sign that you are the provider of food, and therefore the leader/parent, which might help the mealtime sense of security and comfort with your leadership be broadened to other contexts.

Armpit bread

Armpit bread is a slightly offbeat extrapolation of the idea behind hand feeding (above) which brings in the sense of smell to strengthen your dog's identification of you as leader/parent.

It involves taking a slice of bread, wedging it inside your armpit, and leaving it there for a bit to absorb your unique, intimate scent. Most effective if you haven't showered for a while. Then hand the bread to your dog (for him to eat).

This exercise employs the hand-feeding principle of strengthening leadership, but with the enhancement of olfactory identification to solidify the bond – particularly effective given the powerful sense of smell possessed by dogs.

I would avoid doing this too frequently with bread – it's good at absorbing odour, but is a grain-based food so can be tough for dogs to digest properly. But have fun experimenting with other canine-safe foods that feel nice under your arm.

After you

Training your dog to follow you through a door, rather than having him blustering through ahead of you, is a good way to instil a clear message that you are the leader. This can require a great deal of persistence for the more cocksure dogs, and requires him to be proficient with 'sit', 'stay' and 'heel' commands (see the training section at the end of this book).

Have him sit fairly close to a closed door – close enough so you don't have to move away from him to reach out and open the door. Ask him to stay, then reach out and open the door. To begin with, you'll need to do this slowly, and remind him to stay whenever you spot the slightest sign that he might be thinking of moving. If you can get the door open with him still in the sit position, ask him to heel, and walk through the door with him in the heel position. Treat and praise generously once you have got through the door – but only if he is still behind you.

If anything goes wrong – he charges through the door first, or doesn't stay properly, don't treat him. Give him a moment to cool down, then try again. When he gets the hang of it, try with more challenging doors – for example, have him follow you out of the front door of your house.

Closed doors are exciting things for dogs, so if you can train him to follow you calmly through a door you will be very effectively asserting your position as parent/leader.

Routine enforcement

Sharpening up your daily routine can help build your dog's trust and confidence in you. If he knows, for example, that he is always going to get his food shortly after coming home from a walk, or his meal will be served at the same time each day, he will have more confidence in your role as parent/leader.

Routine treats

Get into the habit of giving your dog a favourite treat at the same time each day. When you get home after the evening walk, give a treat, or when you get home from the shops, when the post arrives, etc. It doesn't have to be frequent – one or two times a day is fine, but it helps if it happens at moments which are distinctive and easily recognisable for the dog (not, for example, the start of your favourite TV show). This helps to enforce your position as a generous, reliable parent/leader. Some owners don't like to give an unearned treat, so you can make him earn it by requesting something simple like a 'sit'.

The bucket list

As mentioned earlier in this chapter, guiding your dog through new experiences, situations and places is a strong way to build his trust in your parentship. So, try drawing up a bucket list of new experiences you think would be enriching and enjoyable for your dog, but which take him out of his regular comfort zone a bit. Try to tackle one each weekend/month. The bucket list is also a strategy I advocate for helping dogs with depression – take a look at the depression chapter for some examples of what might be included on a dog's bucket list.

THE RELATIONSHIP TEST

Now that you've done some work on your role as parent/leader for your dog, you might want to measure your relationship against the following possible signs of a strong bond between dog and human.

He predicts your movements

You make your cup of tea, go to sit on the sofa, and find your dog's already on it, waiting patiently for you to arrive. When you get ready for the evening dog walk, he's sat all perky and expectant at the door. These sort of signs suggests that your dog not only knows the routine, but trusts you to follow it. It's probably a good sign of his sense of security in your leadership.

He doesn't go nuts when you return home

If you come home after leaving your dog there alone for a bit, and he gives you a calm nice-to-see-you greeting, this is probably a great sign. A dog who greets you manically has been bouncing off the walls with anxiety, wondering if he's to be alone for ever, expending lots of energy desperately anticipating your return – hence his overly jubilant response when you do finally appear. But a dog who calmly greets has been under no such stress – he trusts, and feels secure in the knowledge, that you will return in good time. He has faith in your parental role in his life, and knows there is nothing to worry about. So don't be disappointed if you get little more than a gentle tail wag when you get back home.

He looks at you

Do you ever notice your dog gazing at you in a way that makes you wonder what he wants? Is he after some food? Or is there something worrying him? If he's making relaxed eye contact with you – his ears, jaw, and facial muscles appear relaxed – then he's looking at you because he's enjoying the feeling of comfort and security he gets from knowing you're nearby. If his face is all tensed up, his ears are back, and perhaps his teeth are bared, then it's not such a good sign!

He looks at you while he's doing a poo

Dogs feel instinctively vulnerable when they squat for a poo. They need someone reliable to keep a lookout for hazards. If he looks at you, it means he trusts you to do this important job. He's watching to see if you make any indication that he might need to urgently cancel his business.

He's a rubber band on walks

If, on an off-lead walk, your dog roams off by himself but often returns to you, and stops at bends or forks in the path to watch for where you want to go, this is a probably a good sign of his trust and confidence in you. He looks to you for direction when he's not sure where to go, rather than making up his own mind. He roams off by himself because he trusts you will be there when he comes back. A dog who clings really closely to the owner might not have this level of confidence. Or, the dog might just be anxious due to the particular surroundings.

He is relaxed

You're relaxing on the sofa in the evening, and your dog is napping at your side. You go to the kitchen to get a cup of tea. When you return, your dog is still peacefully napping. This is probably a good sign that he feels confident and secure in the relationship. A dog who snaps out of his doze whenever you make a movement, and who follows you whenever you go to a different room, might not feel so secure – he can't yet trust that you are not going to abandon him, perhaps.

Take the above signs with a generous pinch of salt – all dogs have their own ways of communicating, so if none of those 'measurements' fit with your dog it does not necessarily mean your relationship is not working well. The only measurement that really matters is your own appreciation of your dog's improved behaviour and comfort.

.

DEPRESSION

DO DOGS GET DEPRESSED?

Short answer: yes. Longer answer: yes, but it's difficult to decipher the extent to which canine depression mirrors the human experience of depression. The emotional machinations of our four-legged friends are still largely undiscovered by veterinary science – because dogs can't talk to psychologists about their feelings.

What we do know

Dogs can feel depressed, and experience similar symptoms of depression as humans. For example: loss of appetite, changes in behaviour, changes in eating and sleeping routines, reduction of activity, withdrawing from activities which they previously enjoyed, and so forth.

Dog depression most often results from an external stimulus – for example, a traumatic change like a house move or death of an owner or companion pet.

What we don't know

Even the most cheerful and active human can be struck down by clinical depression even when there is no external trigger. The chemical makeup and mischief inside our bodies can make us depressed for seemingly no reason. We don't know whether this is also true for dogs. Are our happy-looking pooches secretly suffering from hidden angst and woe that's fuelled by the chemical interactions taking place in their bodies? We don't know.

The signs of dog depression

The signs of depression are not hard to spot – especially when considering how closely they mimic the symptoms of human depression.

- o Loss of appetite.

- o Sleeping more or less than usual.

- o Not wanting to go for walks.

- o A loss of former excitement – for example, no longer getting up to greet an owner who's returned home.

- o Wanting to spend more time alone rather than in the company of humans or other pets in the household.

- o 'Hiding' in obscure, secretive parts of the house.

- o A general demeanour of grumpiness and listlessness in a previously cheerful dog.

The key marker is **change** – a distinct change in the dog's behaviour which has been triggered by an external, traumatic (for the dog) change in the dog's environment.

Crucially, these symptoms of dog depression could also be symptoms of another illness – for example, a dog who suddenly becomes reluctant to exercise may be suffering from the onset of arthritis – so always get a veterinary consult if your dog starts showing these signs of depression.

CHEER UP – IT'S NOT AS BAD AS IT SEEMS

It can be devastating for an owner to have to confront the fact that his/her dog is feeling depressed. What sort of owner could be so terrible that they even manage to make their dog feel miserable?

However, dog depression is an easier form of unhappiness to address than many others, and, depending on the context, it can in fact be a really good sign. A dog who becomes depressed has overcome the need to feel anxious or stressed.

For example, perhaps your dog has been suffering from separation anxiety, and you've been working hard to help him address it. Previously, when you left him home alone, he would spend all his energy being anxious and stressed – barking himself into a frenzy and tearing around the house in a destructive whirlwind.

But now you've helped him, he is no longer stressed or anxious when you leave. He no longer feels the need to spend all morning pacing up and down at the back door, because he feels secure and confident that you will return. As a consequence, there is nothing for him to **do**. He's lost his vocation; he's lost his employment of being all stressed out.

Of course, this is a great thing. It means you've successfully helped your dog overcome his anxiety (wherever it be separation anxiety or something else like territorial aggression). We just need to fill the void that's left behind with a form of fulfilment that's healthier than the one obtained by venting his now-extinguished anxiety. In this sort of context, you've reached the 'next level' and are much closer to having a happy dog.

Alternatively, you might have a dog who's never suffered from anxiety but has started to feel depressed. Perhaps a companion pet has passed away. Perhaps the dog's owner has to travel a lot, and the poor dog suddenly finds himself missing his favourite human. Or perhaps the dog has had to move to a new house and surroundings which he doesn't like as much as his old ones. Either way, don't get too downhearted yourself. Dog depression is actually quite an enjoyable – and invariably successful – issue to overcome.

THE ROOTS OF DOG DEPRESSION

In my experience, dog depression is most commonly triggered by one of these three stimuli: loneliness, lack of fulfilment, and dislike of a new environment. The first two are more common than the third. I am going to deal with loneliness and lack of fulfilment in this section. If a dog dislikes new surroundings to which he has recently been introduced, this can trigger depression as he withdraws to the (often limited) comfort zone and doesn't want to leave it – this might be under the bed, in a cupboard, or wherever he has chosen. It can also result in anxiety – he becomes stressed or aggressive in this new environment. Both need to be treated by making him more comfortable with his new environment, so please refer to ENVIRONMENTAL ANXIETY (p205) for help with this.

Lack of fulfilment

An unsurprising and easy form of dog depression to understand – humans who have nothing fulfilling to do in their lives get depressed, and so do dogs. It's often said that working dog breeds are most prone to this form of depression, but it can occur in any breed if the dog has nothing to do. Dogs whose lives aren't necessarily empty, but who rarely experience anything other than the same routine (walk in the park in the morning and evening, playtime after work, obedience class every Thursday, etc.) can get bored and swept into a dark pit of ennui, whereas other dogs will enjoy familiar routine.

At the very advanced level, this can be overcome by training your dog to do jobs around the house – collecting the laundry, picking up fallen leaves in the garden, etc. But a more accessible solution is to spice up your dog's life in a range of not-necessarily-elaborate ways which we'll look at in this chapter. Essentially, we want to fill his day as much as possible with things for him to **do**.

Loneliness

Common in dogs who have recently lost another family pet or owner, or dogs who have had to move away from a home with canine companions to one without them, depression triggered by loneliness shares close similarity to lack of fulfilment. The dog no longer has anything to do (e.g. playing with his companion) and we, the owner, need to help fill the void. But there is also a need for social fulfilment, and sometimes circumstances don't allow us to provide this by replacing the lost companion. Loneliness can also strike dogs whose owners don't have the time to pay them enough attention – perhaps a new job or new baby has caused a shift in focus.

Modern veterinary discourse explores the emotional pressures placed on dogs as a result of the way human society has evolved. Our modern-day preoccupation with digital technology and social media can mean that domestic dogs have huge competition for their owners' time and attention. Modern dogs' daily lives are also more confining in nature than, say, fifty years ago when it was common for dogs to roam freely beyond the bounds of the house and garden. As owners, we should reflect on how effectively our day-to-day routine accommodates the needs of our dogs, and whether there is any leeway to make things more amenable.

Another thing to consider is how potently dogs reflect the mood of the people in their surroundings. Dogs who live in happy, lively households tend to project the same intensity in their own demeanours. The converse is also true for dogs who live in quieter households, perhaps with a single owner who might suffer from a human form of depression. It might therefore be worthwhile for the owner to address his own emotional wellbeing before attending to his dog's.

FUNDAMENTALS OF DEFEATING DOG DEPRESSION

Our desire is to cheer up the depressed dog by making his daily existence as fulfilling and enjoyable as possible, and in a moment we'll look at some easy ways of achieving this. But let's start with the fundamental principles of tackling depression.

Ensure sound physical health

A reminder: a dog who exhibits signs of depression might in fact be suffering from a physical, rather than emotional, illness – so we mustn't proceed until he's been given the physical 'all clear' by the vet.

Ensure basic needs are being met

These include:

- o Sufficient exercise.

- o A balanced and enjoyable diet which satisfies the dog's nutritional needs.

- o Security – a place in the house which is the dog's own, and where he feels completely comfortable and safe.

- o Companionship – the dog isn't left to his own devices for too long.

Embrace routine

While some individuals may like each new day to be a wild and unpredictable adventure, dogs tend to feel most happy and secure when they have a good sense of routine. Keep walks, mealtimes, training and play sessions at the same approximate time each day.

Be happy

An owner who mopes about in his own sulky stupor can't expect to rescue his dog from similar despair. We need to nurture and exude our own happiness so our dogs will feed off it. (Human) couch potatoes will need to alter and reinvigorate their regimen and bring renewed vibrancy to the household mood.

Create a culture of fulfilment

Don't we (humans) all have a list of things we would like to accomplish in our lifetimes? Our dogs should have a list like this, too. An essential step is to draw up a bucket list for your dog. This might be an annual list, with things to be ticked off over the course of a single year, or a more long-term series of ambitions. Pin it up somewhere visible to help you and your dog keep actively striving to accomplish each goal.

Here are some suggestions for annual or lifetime canine bucket lists:

o   Visit a foreign country.

o   Learn to count from one to ten.

o   Travel on a boat.

o   Participate in a dog show.

o   Watch a sunrise together.

o   Go camping.

o   Go swimming together in the ocean.

o   Go swimming together in three different oceans.

o   Go on a picnic.

o   Give your dog a professional photoshoot.

o   Climb a mountain.

o   Try a raw-food diet.

o   Throw a party for your dog.

o   Visit ten historical landmarks.

o   Visit all the dog-friendly businesses in your region (e.g., have a 'puppachino' at Starbucks and go shopping together in 'Pets at Home').

o   Go on a road trip.

o   Play in the snow.

o   Enter the 'Muddy Dog Challenge' (a UK obstacle course over 2.5 or 5km which you race in a team with your dog) or equivalent.

o   Take your dog to work.

o   Go to agility/obedience classes.

o   Sleep in a (dog-friendly) hotel.

o   Hike a long-distance trail (e.g. Pennine Way in UK, or Greenstone Ridge Trail, MI US).

o   Have a steak dinner.

o   Get pampered at a grooming salon or doggy spa.

o   Play in a ball pool.

o   Go trick or treating.

o   Have a barbeque.

o   Visit a new place every week.

When tailoring your dog's bucket list, look for adventurous, new and enriching experiences that your dog will actually enjoy. Travelling on a plane might seem adventurous, but could be hell for your dog.

Having these concrete goals to work toward will help encourage you to make your dog's life more stimulating and fulfilling in general. Every singe day need not necessarily bring a new adventure, but you'll be looking for opportunities to do something new and fun for both of you.

DOG DEPRESSION: PRACTICAL APPROACHES

Early-morning reluctance

For the owner of a depressed dog, one of the most disheartening moments of the day is the very first one. You're up at the crack of dawn, all keen to go out for the morning dog walk – but Sad Susan over there in her bed merely peers at you disconsolately, refusing to get up and refusing to share your bright spirits. This sort of reluctance to get out of bed and to exercise is a key marker of dog depression (as it is of human depression).

It's easy to tackle this the wrong way: get some treats and use them to lure the sad dog out of bed, calling her name encouragingly and giving heavy praise with relief in your voice when she finally ambles over to collect her reward. The big problem with this approach is that it indulges the dog's sulky behaviour and encourages her to repeat it. She learns that if she is sulky and reluctant first thing in the morning, she will first get the owner's attention and then a food reward.

Instead, we want to show her that morning is a fun time that's worth getting out of bed for. So, we completely ignore the dog as she lays sulking in her bed – no eye contact, nothing spoken to her, no engagement at all. Instead, we're going to go out into the garden and find something interesting and fun to do. Something unpredictable which will hook the dog's interest and make her want to get out of bed to see what's going on.

For some dogs, all we need to do is go outside and hide behind a bush. She'll come out wondering where we've gone and eventually sniff out our hiding place, at which point we can jump up (in a 'fun' way – we don't want to traumatise her) and perhaps have a game of chase around the garden.

Other dogs might need something a bit more noisy and tantalising to get their interest. The owner can go and play the drums on some flower pots, throw some stones into the pond, shake some bushes, or just go and sing in a corner of the garden – anything that gets the dog's interest. Once she's come to investigate, we immediately engage with her in a fun activity – the game of chase, or playing with one of her toys, or a game of catch/fetch. We only engage with her once she's doing the 'right' thing – she's up out of bed and joining in the fun.

This approach doesn't indulge her sulkiness – instead it gives her the stimulation whose lack possibly contributed to her depressed feelings in the first place. It doesn't take long to do; the only challenges for the owner lies in finding the early-morning energy to be stimulating for the dog, and finding a wide enough range of different things to do so it doesn't become predictable – and boring – for the dog. They don't all have to be in the garden. Hide and seek in the house works well, too.

THE MORNING WALK

Now the first step's complete — we've got Sad Susan out of bed; she's out in the garden, tail wagging after her early-morning moment of fun. Accomplishing the next level — getting the depressed dog out for the morning walk — can be a bit more challenging.

An important point here is to get the routine right. If your dog has breakfast, it will most likely be best to leave it until after the walk so it can serve as a form of motivation. Also, it's generally unwise for dogs to exercise immediately after filling their stomachs.

We want to keep up the ethos of providing the depressed dog a fun, stimulating, interesting experience. Ideally, this would mean going out to explore different places for the morning walk. Dogs do become quite easily bored if they go to the same place and the same route every day. Unfortunately, for a lot of owners simply isn't time to head off in the car toward far-flung exotic walking spots first thing in the morning, but we should still make the best of all opportunities open to us. If you normally take the footpath beside your house that heads out across the fields, try taking your dog through the middle of town instead. This will mean more on-lead walking and perhaps less intense physical exercise, but the different sights, sounds and experience will stimulate her. Even just having two or three different possibilities for the morning walk can provide enough variety to make your dog interested in what experiences the morning walk may bring.

It's easier to bring more variety to the experience of the walk itself, even if you can't vary the location of the walk. If your dog's used to off-lead roaming around the fields or forest, try some on-lead walking, with 'heel' practice, instead. Throw in some practice of other training exercises like 'sit' and 'stay'. Keep the pace of the walk varied — see 'the power walk' in the previous 'Leadership

Anxiety' section. Bring a toy on the walk. Anything to avoid your dog thinking the morning walk is going to be the exact same plod as it was yesterday.

If you can arrange to walk your dog along with a fellow dog owner, that would of course be ideal as it gives the lonely dog some of the socialisation of which she might feel a lack. If your dog is anxious of other dogs, or you yourself are worried about other dogs getting near your own, work toward breaking down some barriers. Don't fall into the complacency of avoiding other dogs on the morning walk (unless they really are vicious beasts). Help your dog to overcome any fear-induced anxiety of others so that she can enjoy some morning socialisation.

The above steps are all well and good if you can actually get the dog out through the back gate in the first place, but it's often the first few steps of the walk that can be most challenging. I knew an owner of a Newfoundland who had to physically push his 70kg dog through the gate and up the road just to get him moving; once the first few yards were done the dog would quite happily trot along on his own steam. Some steps we can take to get through those tricky first steps include:

o   Using treats to tantalise the dog forward.

o   Using a well-practised 'heel' command, rewarding with treats when the dog complies.

o   Try taking pressure off the dog by removing the focus of attention from her. Pretend to have a talk on your mobile phone (while keeping mindful of everyone's safety!) and look away from the dog while doing so. This might make it more comfortable for the dog to get started on her walk.

- o Enlist the help of another dog walker. Your depressed dog will likely be more keen to start the walk if canine company is present.

With very reluctant dogs, you have to get a bit creative – and a bit silly. I find the most effective way to get a dog moving is to make her intrigued in what I am doing, and make her want to follow me. For example, I will crouch low on the floor and pretend to investigate something really interesting. Or I will 'hide' behind a bush. Or I'll put on a show of excitement, jumping up and down a bit and allowing the dog to share my excitement. Unusual, unpredictable actions (which won't trigger anxiety) work really well at engaging the dog's interest and making her want to follow along. Once we've got up a bit of steam, I switch to more conventional ways of making the walk stimulating – chucking a toy around, doing some powerwalking, etc.

With time, the dog learns that the morning walk is going to be full of interest and will be much more keen to get going.

MEALTIME

Reminder: loss of appetite in a dog can indicate physical illness; only proceed here once your dog's had the physical all-clear from the vets.

Whilst many dogs get hugely excited at mealtimes, it's not uncommon for a dog to be uninterested in his food, or to be not very food motivated. Often a dog who is feeling depressed will lose his previous interest in food. It's the change in behaviour which is the indication of depression – a dog who has always just not been particularly excited about food need not necessarily be suffering from depression.

Mealtimes provide an excellent opportunity to give the depressed dog a needed boost to his fulfilment and stimulation – and even dogs who aren't depressed might get some satisfaction from the suggestions in this section. Where food is concerned, we look to tackle some of the redundancy which plagues the lifestyle of the modern domestic dog. Many of his animalistic, primeval features are not needed, or are undesirable, in modern society. He does not need to use his outstanding sense of smell and powerful body to hunt or scavenge his food; it is served up in a bowl for his ease and convenience. He does not need to put those magnificent teeth to use in tearing up hunks of flesh; his modern food comes in little bitesize biscuits which only need the most cursory crunching.

Although we might expect our dogs to appreciate the convenience of this modern, easy lifestyle, it actually removes a lot of their sense of purpose and enjoyment. The hunt, the scavenge, the tearing up of food is what gives them satisfaction, endorphins, fulfilment and enjoyment. So, in particular with the depressed dog, our aim is to remove some of this modern convenience and replace mealtimes with a more primal means of receiving food. In a moment, we'll look at how to approach this in ways that aren't hugely inconvenient for the owner. But first let's consider the actual nature of the depressed dog's diet, and whether we need to change it.

Dietary adjustments

When a dog loses interest in his food, the immediate temptation for the owner is to find a different food which reinvigorates his mealtime excitement. However, this may not be the best action to take. Unlike humans, they don't look for a variety of tastes in their food. Provided the type of food they receive gives them the necessary sustenance, and is reasonably tasty, they will be happy with it. Any changes can upset their sense of stable routine, and can cause unnecessary disturbance to their digestive systems. It is better to look for changes to the actual event of mealtime, rather than to the food itself.

Having said that, there are some changes to the food which could be helpful. It's important to check that the brand of food you are feeding is of good nutritional quality. There are some superb sites on the internet which review all dog foods and give them a quality rating (search for 'dog food reviews' or 'all about dog food'). You might be surprised at the rating your dog's brand gets, especially if it's a supermarket-shelf variety. A bit of research can lead to a much better, and not necessarily more expensive, brand of food which may boost your dog's general wellbeing.

Texture and consistency can be important to a lot of dogs – sometimes more than flavour. If he doesn't seem to be enjoying dry food, you might give wet food a try (and vice versa). Wet food can cause the build up of plaque on teeth, so offer bones or dental chews/toys after meals.

Speaking of bones – these are one of the greatest dietary enhancements you can make. Chewing on a bone is great for the teeth, but it also engages the dog with his primal roots. It is a more natural form of nutritional intake for him. Chewing is good for jaw health and releases endorphins, so you should definitely consider offering bones to a dog who is feeling depressed. Just make sure you give him the right sort of bone.

In pet shops, you will find cooked bones but these should never be given to a dog. They can be too hard and cause damage to the teeth, or too brittle which means bits of hard, cooked bone will get into the gut and cause damage there. Dogs are designed for ingesting raw bones, so these are what should be offered.

Raw chicken bones are a good way to start – try wings for a small dog, necks for a medium-sized dog, and carcasses for a large dog. Chicken bones are too soft to clean teeth though, so you'll want to work up to something harder like raw lamb or raw beef bones.

The best raw bones have meat on them – these are known as RMBs, or raw meaty bones. There is no need to worry about giving your dog raw meat; their internals, unlike human intestines, are well-equipped to cope with bacteria such as salmonella. After a few sessions with chicken bones, his digestive system should have no trouble coping with firmer bones.

Raw lamb ribs, backs, necks and legs are good choices. I also give beef rib and marrow bones to larger dogs who are already used to raw bones. Avoid knuckle bones as these can be too hard for the teeth to tackle. It is generally best to avoid weight-bearing beef bones, as they can also be too hard. The hardness gradient goes from chicken bones (softest) to lamb bones, to pork bones, to beef bones (hardest). When selecting your dog's bone, verge on the large side. It is best for him to have a big bone that he can get to work on than a small bone which might not be crunched up into small enough pieces. A common guidance is to choose bones which are no smaller than the head of the dog who will be eating it; I'm not sure this is particularly helpful as most bones aren't shaped like a dog's head so it's hard to compare size.

One good, tasty and healthy way to make your dog's main meal more tantalising is to add a meat stock to it. The enhanced taste, and especially smell, might help to get him excited over the meal. Bone broth can work really well for this. Be wary of using gravy powder mixes as these can have high salt content.

Re-inventing the meal

There's a massive clash between what we – humans – consider a meal experience to be, and what dogs consider it should be. For us, it's sitting down to a delicately arranged plate of food which we navigate with fine cutlery and punctuate with polite conversation. For dogs, it is (or once was) a hunt – a chase after some unfortunate animal – or a frantic scavenge for food, full of energy and excitement, necessitating the use of their precise olfactory powers and exercising their strong jaws. But that visceral delight is lost for the modern domestic dog. We have enforced our more sedate meal time arrangements onto our canine counterparts, presenting them with a bowl of food we've arranged for them. They haven't had to work for it; they get it without the buzz of a furious hunt beforehand. For the depressed dog, we can re-introduce some of the primal joy and excitement that his ancestors would have associated with food.

So we need to adjust our perception of what mealtime should be for our dogs. Not a quiet, sedentary affair, but an energetic activity which gets his redundant primal features back in employment.

Adjusting routine so your dog has his meal soon after an energetic walk can help. It partially recaptures the association between the exercise of the hunt and the reward of the food. He goes for a walk, gets all the exercise, and then has his food afterwards. It almost feels like a proper hunt. If your dog currently has his meal a long time after his walk, you'll probably find he is noticeably more receptive to his food if you rearrange schedule in this way. Just be a bit careful if you have a large breed of dog, or another type of dog that is susceptible to bloat. In these cases, it is best to leave a bit of time after the exercise for the body to settle, and then give the meal.

With the meal itself – a good starting step to try is to place some 'obstacles' in your dog's dinner bowl. A couple of tennis balls work well, though you might need something smaller depending on the size of dog/bowl. Even something so simple as this goes some way to replicate the feeling of a hunt/scavenge. Having to work through the obstacle, using his nose and snout, will stimulate him and make him feel as if he is 'hunting' for his food – at least a little bit. It has the added benefit of slowing down the ingestion speed, which can be great for dogs who upset their stomachs by eating too quickly.

Pet shops sell special 'food mazes' which serve the same purpose. These are plastic fittings that sit at the bottom of the bowl and they have the shape of a maze, or random lumps and bumps, which make the dog work harder for his food. They are marketed as ways to slow down eating, but for many dogs they make the mealtime experience more fulfilling because the dog must be more physically and mentally engaged in the eating activity.

There are other excellent ways to give your dog more of this physical engagement during mealtimes – but most involve doing away with the concept of the dog's dinner bowl. A superb product is the KONG 'Wobbler'. This is a self-righting large plastic toy with a small hole in the side. You open it up and put food inside it. As the dog knocks it with his feet or snout, it will dispense food through the small hole. This is a great simulation of the hunt experience and most dogs will really enjoy getting their meal in this way. However, it only works well with dry food, and you will need to help your dog learn how to use it at first – but he should catch on pretty quickly.

Why do we give our dogs their food in a bowl? Is it for them, or for us? Why not try using a different container? I suggest your garden lawn. This will be perfectly safe provided you haven't sprayed your lawn with any chemical treatment. It won't matter if he eats a bit of grass or dirt along with his food. I sometimes like to go out into my garden and chuck handfuls of my dogs' food across the grass. They enjoy sniffing it out. It allows them to use their sense of smell and rewards them with food – a fulfilling hunt/scavenge-like experience. Cleanliness can be a disadvantage for the owner, but most dogs will spend much time and energy happily covering the whole garden until they are sure they've got every crumb.

The lawn-scattered meal works for wet or dry food, but if you're using wet you might try freezing it in ice-cube shapes beforehand. Take them out of the freezer before they get too hard, so your dog doesn't damage his teeth on them. This makes the food more convenient to throw around, but can also quite surprisingly make the food more enjoyable to eat. A lot of dogs enjoy the consistency of partially-frozen food.

Owners who want to make mealtime a more contained affair can still look for over varieties of container instead of the conventional bowl. Cardboard boxes are brilliant. Look for ones which will make it tricky for your dog to access food placed inside. Narrow breakfast cereal boxes work well. Best served outside, the food-filled cardboard box will provide great stimulation for your dog. He will have to work out how to get at the food, and may decide to tear up the box. He'll enjoy this. Supervise and make sure he's not eating too much of the actual cardboard. The shredded remains can still be recycled.

Step up the physical aspect by fixing a decent length of string to the food-filled box (or other container). You hold the other end of the string, and run around your garden. Now your dog has a prey which he must hunt. Such a close approximation to the primal hunt is going to be hugely stimulating for a lot of dogs, even depressed ones, and getting the owner more actively involved in the mealtime experience will strengthen the relationship. For owners who can't do too much running, simply tie the string to the end of a broom. Now you can stand still in the middle of the garden and just wave the broom around – the combination of the broom handle and string gives plenty of reach. It's a bit of hassle to set up, but if you're willing to go to the trouble, your dog will have a wonderfully fulfilling mealtime which gives superb exercise for his prey drive. Remember that dogs shouldn't eat immediately after vigorous exercise, so don't let things get too frenzied!

For a less troublesome way of initiating his prey drive at mealtime, simply hide his food (in its normal boring bowl) somewhere and let him sniff it out. He'll need some encouragement and hints the first couple of times, but will soon catch on to the game and enjoy using his nose to hunt down his dinner.

Making mealtimes more physical and stimulating, and aiming to give some exercise for the dog's primal hunter/scavenger instincts, is a very effective way to help a depressed dog, but can make any dog's daily life more fulfilling. The above suggestions are my favourite methods, but there are countless other ways for the imaginative dog owner to make mealtime more stimulating.

OTHER TIMES OF THE DAY

We've looked at ways of helping a depressed dog during the mealtime and the dog walk, but what about the gaps of day between these events? A depressed dog might spend more time sleeping than is normal for him, which is perhaps preferable to the destructive or harmful behaviour of an anxious dog – but the owner's challenge is in finding enough things to give him a good degree of fulfilment.

If your depressed dog is a recovered separation-anxiety sufferer, you'll want to continue providing him with a varied range of stimulating activities as we covered in the 'Separation Anxiety' chapter. If your dog has not suffered separation anxiety, it would still be worth consulting that chapter as the suggested activities will help bring stimulation and fulfilment to your depressed dog.

Time is precious

It is not difficult or time consuming to knock up some quick activities that can be really good fun for a dog; we'll look at some in a moment. Perhaps the owner's biggest difficulty is making enough time, in a busy working/family life, to engage with the dog through playtime and training. Many much-loved and well-cared-for dogs can become a little withdrawn and depressed simply because their owners, despite feeding their dogs properly and going to the vets regularly, are simply too busy to give enough attention to their pets. This is nothing to feel bad about – it is a difficult pitfall to avoid with modern lifestyles. But it does mean that a crucial step in helping depressed dogs is for owners to look carefully at their daily schedule and work hard to free up even just a little bit more good-quality time where they, or their family members, can engage with the dog without distraction.

This time can be spent on work (training) or play. Your dog will really enjoy some regular training sessions, and these will strengthen the owner/dog relationship, as well as the dog's general behaviour, if you can keep them regular. Have a look at the training section at the end of this book for some things you can start working on.

Playtime, however, is just as valuable – especially if the owner has time to join in. The activities in following in this section, and the ones in the separation-anxiety chapter, can be enjoyed by the dog alone if no time is available, but nothing can beat something even so simple as a tug of war, or a game of fetch, shared between dog and owner.

If your dog has been suffering depression, it might seem as if he isn't the slightest bit interested in playing, or doesn't know how to play. Any toy waggled in front of his face or tantalisingly bounced ball is met with his sombre, disinterest. So we need to give him a lesson about how to play, and reinvigorate his puppyhood pleasure for playtime.

Training to play

Start by choosing a toy which can be used to train your dog to play. If there's a toy which he seems the slightest bit interested in, go for that; otherwise, pick anything safe – but keep using the same one for these training sessions. If, for some reason, there's no dog toys available, grab an old sock or something safe which you don't mind him getting his mouth around.

Have in hand some of your dog's favourite treats, and approach him with the toy. Show it too him; try and make it look interesting. Squeaky toys work well, or toys which you can get some sort of sound out of. Do whatever you can to get your dog's attention on the toy. Your aim is to reward him – with the treats and verbal praise – as soon as he shows (even the slightest sign of) interest in the toy.

Some keener dogs will immediately want to get their mouth around the toy – great; offer a treat and praise him. Few dogs will be able to resist at least looking at the toy, so long as you're making it seem reasonably interesting. As soon as his eyes fix on it, praise and treat him.

Keep building on this. Praise and treat your dog whenever he shows any sign of interest in the toy. He'll soon start to build positive association with the toy; he'll want to show interest in it.

Work toward the point where he's getting it in his mouth, keeping the praise and treats flowing generously. Soon, you should be able to start having a game of sorts – a tug of war, or tossing the toy for him to fetch. He'll start having fun. Congratulations – you've taught (or reminded) your dog how to play!

FUN FOR TWO

Let's build on the playtime success by trying some stimulating and fun things that dog and human can enjoy together.

First, football (or soccer). You can train your dog to play football in a similar way to the method described above. Do you ever spot him tapping a ball with his paws? If so, start catching these moments. Whenever you spot his paw coming into contact with the ball, immediately praise and treat him. This has to be quick – any delay between paw contact and reward makes it difficult for him to understand what he's being rewarded for. A clicker helps immensely (with this, and with many other exercises). With enough repetitions, he'll get the idea that he is rewarded for touching the ball with his paw. He'll start touching it more energetically, so start getting more selective and only reward when his paw 'kicks' the ball. Now add a command word – ask your dog to "kick" the ball; reward when he does so and keep building the association between command word and action. Now you can enjoy a game of football with your dog. Why not take it further? Set up a goal and reward him whenever he 'scores'. Maybe one day you'll manage to teach him the offside rule...

A more straightforward activity, which is good for enticing a reluctant player, is hide and seek. This fuels the intrigue of even the most quiet and still dog. When you're sitting with your dog (watching the TV, relaxing together in the garden, etc.) just get up and leave. If he doesn't follow you, he will almost certainly be watching you. Don't worry if not. Find somewhere to hide in or around your house. Don't make it too difficult on a first attempt.

You may or may not need to call and encourage your dog to find you. Try not calling him first. Just patiently wait in your hiding spot. Eventually, even reticent dogs will be too intrigued and will come to find you – hopefully he will manage this reasonably easily, provided you've not been too stealthy with your hiding. Give him lots of praise and a treat once he's tracked you down.

If you've been waiting for ages and he's still not come to find you, then he'll need some encouragement. Calling his name might work. Or, you could use a smelly object (an open jar of peanut butter, hunk of cheese, etc.). When the scent has guided him to you, reward him with a bit of the peanut butter/cheese.

After a few repetitions, your dog will soon understand the idea behind the game and will likely be a bit more energetic in seeking you out. Have fun with the game – it will always be stimulating for him, and the moment of joy when he finds you will give extra strength to the relationship.

Hide and seek is a good starter game for reluctant players. Once he's practised with that, a game of chase is a good way to step up the activity levels – and requires a bit more physical activity form the owner. This is one of my personal favourite games (I think my dogs enjoy it too!). It works best if you have something like a shed or reasonably large bush/shrubbery, which you can get all around, in your garden. When you're out in the garden with your dog, simply dash away from him and 'hide' behind the shed/bush. As you hear him coming to follow you, quickly move further around the shed/bush, away from him. He'll likely pause for a moment, wondering where you've gone or what on earth you're up to, before continuing on his way around the shed/bush to track you down. Keep moving around the shed and away from him as he pursues you. You'll likely need to get quite fast on your feet. See how long you can last before he catches you (at which point praise and reward him). When he understands the game, he'll anticipate your movements and change direction in his attempts to catch you, so stay sharp! It's a simple game that can be huge fun for all, and has a lot of bonding potential.

Get some toys involved in your shared playtime. Many owners, including me, spend a fair bit of money lavishing their dogs with a wide arsenal of pet-shop toys which never receive much interest from the dog. There's actually no need to spend any money here. I tend to find my dogs' favourite toys are things they find around the house. Items of clothing are popular – old work ties or socks – because they have the owner's smell on them, so can be good for tug of war or chase. One of my dogs had a fondness for plastic bottles. I tied one of them to a piece of string, then I would run across the garden towing the bottle so it becomes something to hunt for the dog. This is a really energetic and stimulating way to engage the prey drive. Play involving toys tends to be lukewarmly received by dogs who are out of the habit of playing, so it will likely be best to start with the hide and seek or chase activities above.

And it's 'habit' which is a key element. Depressed dogs are often simply out of the habit of playing, so by training him to play, and practising the art of play with him, you'll reintroduce some of the stimulation and enjoyment whose lack contributed to the depression in the first place. Even if you have very little time available, a little can go a long way. One game of chase around the shed before/after work can do a lot to boost his mood, especially if you can make it a routine part of his day.

FUN FOR ONE

Wouldn't we love to spend all our day just mucking about and playing with our dogs? They'd love it too. But we shouldn't feel guilty for the harsh time constraints modern life puts on dog owners. What we can do is arrange a few activities that can give our dogs some stimulation and fulfilment during parts of the day when we simply can't engage directly with them.

Let's look at a few activities which don't require a huge amount of preparation and inconvenience on the owner's part. However, it does help if you can gather just a few materials. Have a kitchen cupboard or somewhere you can stock the following items:

- o   newspaper

- o   scrap paper

- o   string

- o   cardboard boxes

- o   cardboard tubes (toilet roll tubes, and kitchen paper tubes)

- o   plastic bottles.

Those few materials can lead to all sorts of different ways to entertain your dog solo, and they are easily amassed in most family households. You can still recycle them once your dog's finished with them. The first times you try these activities, supervise your dog to make sure he's not eating something inappropriate.

Cardboard tubes

Take one of your dog's favourite treats and put it inside a cardboard tube. Wedge it in the middle of the tube with screwed up paper each side. Leave one or two of these treat-loaded tubes around the house where your dog might stumble across them. This will give his prey drive some good stimulation as he uses his smell and teeth to free the treat. Hide the tubes in different and progressively more challenging locations.

Lucky dip

Take a decently sized cardboard box and fill it with shredded or screwed up paper. Now toss a few of your dog's treats into the box, and shake it up so the treats get hidden among the paper. Leave the box somewhere it will pique your dog's interest. He'll have a very jolly and stimulating time sniffing out the treats. Unless he gets really wild, you'll be able to reuse the box and paper for future games.

Bottle puzzle

Take a plastic bottle, open the lid, and drop a treat in it. Voila — this could keep your dog occupied for ages. Just remember to supervise on the first occasions; make sure your dog's not actually ingesting parts of the bottle. Smelly treats work best to engage confused dogs. If it's too difficult, make a few more holes in bottle. Try with other containers like an old cereal box.

Advanced bottle puzzle

For this, make two holes on opposite sides of a plastic bottle, about one-third down the bottle's height from the top. Thread a length of string through the holes, and tie each end to something firm – two sturdy chairs might work – so the string is taut. You should have a tight string which allows the bottle to spin around on it. Put a couple of treats in the bottle and watch your dog's fun ensue.

Treasure hunt

Screw up some balls of old newspaper or scrap paper with some treats inside. Hide them around the house (make it easy to start with). This sort of activity is great for stimulating prey drives and giving your dog a rewarding sense of fulfilment.

These activities are easy to put together and can be left lying around the house for your dog to enjoy when he's not got you available for entertainment. Using a couple of them each day will help step up your dog's general sense of fulfilment.

GAINFUL EMPLOYMENT

Just as people can succumb to depression if they don't have some form of fulfilling employment, a lot of dogs can be caused to feel down if they don't have a sense of purpose. Again, the lifestyle of the modern domestic dog makes redundant some of the behaviours and functions which may be inherent to the breed and species. These days, most dogs don't need to protect their masters from dangerous predators, or round up sheep, or rescue sailors who've fallen overboard. Their form of employment is gone, but the urge to fulfil their employment remains dormant and hungry.

Perhaps your depressed dog could be uplifted if he was given a job to do. Some dogs might be offended at the thought – but it might work for yours. Having something which he knows is his 'thing' to do can be very powerful in making his daily life more fulfilling.

Of course, the tricky bit here is finding an appropriate form of employment for your dog. It is possible to get very ambitious; in my book *Train Your Dog to Read*, I look at how you can train your dog to do household jobs such as collecting the laundry and putting it in the washing machine, or tidying up toys. It takes quite a bit of training to get to that point, however. Here, let's consider other forms of employment which don't have quite such demanding apprenticeships.

When choosing employment, we look for something fulfilling and purposeful for our dog. However, what he considers purposeful may not seem purposeful to us. We can create jobs which don't really need to be done, but he will still feel great about accomplishing them.

Living scarecrow

This one can be easy to train, even for depressed and reluctant dogs – but it does come with a couple of risks. The living scarecrow role involves your dog protecting the garden from pigeons, or other birds, or other unwanted animal intruders like rabbits, possums, etc. Whenever he spots a pigeon in the vicinity, his job is to fly out into the garden and chase it away.

This is a noisy, energetic job which most employees absolutely love. It engages those primal instincts of protection, and is a really fulfilling role. However, there are some obvious disadvantages and risks. Neighbours may not enjoy the noise, for one thing. But it can also encourage dogs to become too territorial. They may be tempted to widen their repertoire and start protecting the garden from other 'intruders' like the mail person, visiting friends, the family cat, and so forth.

This can be circumvented by training. When preparing your dog for this form of employment, you only want to reward him when he chases off the correct intruder: the pigeon. Any inappropriate choices on his part can be met with negative punishment – you put him indoors to temporarily deprive him of his freedom and employment (a short period of unpaid suspension). When he does chase off the correct intruder, this should be met with generous praise and reward. Even when he is well practised and reliable with his employment, he should still be praised and rewarded with reasonable frequency – be a fair boss, and encourage his consistency. Be reasonably persistent with the training, but if he seems incapable of selecting 'intruders' appropriately, it is probably best to consider alternative employment.

It's a simple job to train. For some dogs, all you'll need to do is be present when he spots a pigeon and reward him when he chases it. For less excitable dogs, be ready to praise and reward whenever he shows any sign of interest in an intruding pigeon – just turning his head to look at it, for example. Keep encouraging and building this interest, and he'll eventually be launching himself energetically into the garden. You can add a command word once he's got a good idea of the action you want him to perform.

Some dogs might become workaholics and spend every hour of the day on guard in the garden, so make sure he's not being overworked.

Paper shredder

This job is less 'risky' than the scarecrow. Unless you have sensitive documents that need to be destroyed, it doesn't really serve much of a practical function – though your dog doesn't need to know that. It simply involves placing any waste paper in a special box rather than sending it straight to the recycling bin. When your dog notices there is something in this box, his job is to rip it all to pieces. Then it can go into recycling.

Disadvantage: it can get messy, and will probably mean you will have to clean up lots of shredded paper. But when you see the amount of enjoyment and fulfilment it gives your dog, you probably won't mind. Having something like this to do on a fairly regular basis can give a huge boost to a depressed dog. And with careful training, you can reduce the amount of mess involved.

To train your dog for this role, simply show him to where the box will be located. Avoid changing its position once you've chosen a spot. If it's always in the same place, this will help him understand that only what is in that specific place is to be shredded, and will prevent him going on a free-roaming paper rampage around the house. Encourage his interest by praising and rewarding when he sniffs at the paper, when he picks up the paper, and when he tears it up. Quieter, older dogs will take some time to build up the interest levels but should get there with patience and persistence. Once he's got the idea, you can improve his tidiness by only rewarding when he doesn't take paper away from the box to shred.

If you like, you can add a command word – or perhaps have a little bell to ring – for whenever you put something in the shredding box, so he knows to come and sort it out.

Gardener

Possibly a more seasonal role, and suitable if you have something like a vegetable patch in your garden which needs to be kept free of weeds but doesn't actually have anything precious growing in it for part of the year. However, don't use this form of employment if you treat your garden with chemicals, or have bulbs planted which your dog might swallow.

When you're out weeding in this bit of your garden, encourage your dog to join in. If he's a keen digger, praise and reward when he digs in the correct part of the garden. If he doesn't like to dig, bury a treat (shallowly) in the dirt, and give him plenty of praise when he digs for it. Add your 'dig' command word to help encourage him further.

You'll soon have an enthusiastic assistant at your side when you go out to weed the garden. Keep the praise enthusiastic and consistent so he is encouraged to only dig in the correct area. He might become an independent gardener, and enjoy going to work out there by himself, or he might just want to help you when you're weeding too.

There's no limit to the sorts of employment you can offer your dog; if he's willing, you can train him to do some quite advanced (and possibly even helpful) things. But the main purpose is giving him a sense of purpose, and helping to counter the redundancy of the modern dog – a big contributor of canine depression.

DOG DEPRESSION: CONCLUDING REMARKS

Hopefully, this chapter has given you a range of approaches to try and lift your dog out of his depression. But let's not forget the fundamentals: for a dog to be happy, he needs to be stimulated and fulfilled. Helping a depressed dog really boils down to getting out there and enjoying life with him. Share a rich variety of walks and experiences, and, crucially, fulfil his social needs. If you have a single dog, take him to places where he can socialise – with other dogs and people. Make regular trips to a park that is popular with dogs, and don't shy away from allowing him off-lead socialisation with dogs who are safe. Take him to obedience or agility classes where he can socialise (a lot of owners don't much care about the obedience aspect at these classes; they solely go to give their dog some time with friends). Dogs are often mirrors of their owners. A dog who is depressed or unfulfilled may be an indication that the owner needs to make his own life more fulfilling, or perhaps address his own tendencies toward depression. .

Associative-memory anxiety

Associative-memory anxiety is the term I use for the anxiety triggered by an object or situation which the dog associates with pain, distress, and other negative feelings. You might have had the experience of approaching another walker and dog while out on a walk, only to find that this dog cowers away from you in fear. 'Oh, he's afraid of men (or women)', the owner tells you, so you slink away feeling guilty about your outrageously apparent manliness (or womanliness). This is a classic example of associative-memory anxiety. In the past, some rotten man or woman has been unpleasant to that dog, for whom a man (or woman) is now a symbol of unpleasantness.

The above example is an easily identifiable example of associative-memory anxiety, but it is not always so conspicuous and can be triggered by a limitless range of different objects and situations. Here are some more examples of things that I have known to be associative triggers of anxiety in dogs:

- o men with beards

- o fairly large cardboard boxes or similarly sized and shaped containers

- o balloons (inflated)

- o the sound of fireworks and gunshots

- o opened car boots

- o walking on linoleum or vinyl flooring

- o the sound of music from a radio

- o being in particular rooms in the house, such as the bathroom

- o suitcases

- o the smell of toast

- o the sound of young children crying

- o alarm clocks

- o sticks and anything stick shaped

- o and many others.

There's often a sad story behind the trigger. For example, I worked with one rescued dog who always got very anxious when their owner's alarm clock sounded in the morning. The owner was convinced this was because the dog had been terrified of his previous master, and associated the alarm sound with unpleasant treatment which would interrupt the relative peace of night time.

Associative-memory anxiety can be a compounding factor in other anxieties. A dog who suffers separation anxiety may associate the sight of a briefcase being set down near the front door with the distress of his owner's imminent absence. A dog who exhibits fear-induced anxiety when he notices other dogs in the park may have been attacked in the past, and comes to associate other dogs as a sign of pain. However, associative-memory anxiety can quite easily be mistaken for straightforward, rational fear. If your dog is startled when you open an umbrella, it might not mean he has been subjected to unpleasant umbrella-related experiences in his past — he is probably just taken aback by the sudden and noisy fabric apparition.

It is worth questioning to what extent your dog needs to overcome associative memory anxiety. If a dog is frightened by balloons, the owner can just find another way to celebrate his birthday. If he gets anxious whenever you approach unknown dogs, you can simply turn around and walk him away from them. Although it's a shame for him to miss out on the social aspect of his life, you might decide, for your particular dog, this is the best way to ensure his general happiness and wellbeing. But if your dog has triggers which cannot be easily avoided in his day-to-day life, then we of course want to help him with them.

A good, solid bond between dog and owner is really important for successfully helping with associative-memory anxiety. The 'Leadership Anxiety' section will help you firm up this bond so check there if needed before proceeding.

Overcoming associative-memory anxiety (which I'll refer to as 'AMA') involves the same general principles and methods no matter what sort of trigger your dog recognises. We need to handle it sensitively, because helping dogs to reconfigure their associations can cause distress if they are pushed too hard. We'll look at these methods later in the chapter, but let's start by thinking about how dogs' memories operate so we can get a better understanding of what we're dealing with.

WHAT DOGS REMEMBER

What did you do last weekend? How was your holiday last summer? Did you do anything special to celebrate your birthday last year?

The chances are that you wouldn't have much difficulty answering any of those questions with pretty specific detail. You could probably recall the name of the restaurant you went to on Saturday night, what the waiter looked like, the colour of the wallpaper, and so on. You can do that because as a human, you possess a type of memory which many other mammals, including dogs, can not readily access. It's called episodic memory, so named because it allows you to remember specific episodes in your past. Episodic memory allows us to mentally travel back in time, recreating past events and places in our minds.

Although recent studies are seeking to question it, our current canine understanding tells us that dogs have a very limited episodic memory and can't remember anything specific beyond a few minutes into the past. Rather sadly, he won't remember the fun game of fetch you played with him this morning before you left for work, or the special treat you gave him yesterday just for being such an outlandishly good boy. At least, he won't remember them like you or I do, but in a rather different way.

What dogs use for anything beyond very short-term recall is their associative memory. He remembers thigs by forming emotional associations with the people, objects, places, smells, etc. that fill his world. His association of you is that of a fun, loving owner who plays fetch and gives generous treats. While he doesn't remember every specific game of fetch or treat for very long, every time you play it strengthens this association. And it is strong, functioning like our associations with language. We learn that the word 'cat' associates with a four-legged, pointy-eared animal that is different to a dog, and it's very hard for that association to be broken down. It becomes similarly difficult for your dog to lose the association of you as being a really great person.

But, of course, the same thing works in less positive situations. The dog who is abused as a puppy comes to associate people with pain, and it is an association strengthened by the length and vehemence of the abuse.

What's really interesting, is that due to the weakness of dogs' episodic memories, it is difficult for them to remember *why* they have a particular association for something. When the dog gets terrified of the man in the park who's carrying a stick, he's not actually thinking back to his previous, monstrous, stick-wielding and abusive owner. He doesn't know *why* he's frightened now. He is just responding to the emotional association, without remembering the horrors which gave birth to it.

This episodic weakness makes it easier for us to reconfigure the negative association into something more positive.

TRIGGER AND CONTEXT

So, our task with the AMA-stricken dog is to redesign the negative association he holds for a particular object or situation. The first step is to get an absolutely crystal-clear understanding of what exactly triggers the dog's anxiety. Is he frightened of all men in the park, or is it just men of a certain height/build/colour? Is he frightened of all people wearing a red hat, or is it just red flatcaps that upset him? Observe closely whenever your dog's AMA is triggered and build your knowledge of the trigger's specific details. It might even help to record observations in a notebook. This is important because it's your insight into your dog's mind. We can't help him effectively unless we understand precisely what triggers the anxiety.

My approach when working with AMA dogs is to break down whatever stimulus triggers the anxiety into two separate elements, which I call 'trigger' and 'context'.

The trigger is the object, the physical thing, itself – which we have now clearly defined. For example, the trigger is a man wearing a red hat.

The context is what has to be going on around the red hat man for the dog's anxiety to be triggered. If the dog only gets anxious when he sees a red-hatted man in the woods, then the woods is the context and the man is the trigger. Often, the context has to be quite specific for the anxiety to be triggered. If he saw a red-hatted man in town where there's a lot of noise and activity going on in the context, his anxiety might not be triggered or at least might not be so potent as when the context is the quiet lonely woods. In some cases, however, context has no impact and must be disregarded. Sometimes, context may be everything and there might be no specific trigger object. An example with this is when a dog gets anxious in the morning, because he associates that time of day with his owner's imminent departure and absence. The AMA is compounded by separation anxiety; overcoming the separation anxiety as I laid out earlier in the book will have the eventual effect of reshaping that negative association into something more positive. Addressing the leadership anxiety which itself often compounds separation anxiety will also diminish the effects of the latter. See how complex the web of anxieties can get!

When overcoming our dog's AMA, we're going to need to make use of the trigger object, and it must be kept constant. So we always use as close an approximation to the man in the red hat as we possibly can, exactly the same man in the hat who triggers the anxiety. Context, however, we can vary, and this allows us to approach the reshaping of association in a more gentle, comfortable way for the dog. In my example, we take the man in the red hat and put him in a different context to the woods. We choose a context where the AMA seems to be absent or less powerful, such as the garden. Our aim is to find the least threatening context for the dog to start with. If the anxiety is triggered in your home or garden, try to find somewhere else your dog feels comfortable to begin with – out on his favourite walk, or at the park perhaps. The practicalities can sometimes be tricky – in my example, we need to have a red hat wearing man available. But we must recreate the trigger as accurately as possible, and choose our context carefully.

Safety is something we must not forget to be mindful of, especially when dealing with human triggers. The 'ideal method' outlined below aims for the dog never to feel anxiety, but it is best to have him wear a muzzle just in case. The training section at the end of the book shows you how to help your dog get comfortable with a muzzle if he is not used to wearing one.

CONDITIONING

Our trigger and context are set up, so we can start conditioning our dog's association with the trigger and make it more pleasant. The conditioning process is fairly similar to the one we use for dogs with fear-induced anxiety, but with an important difference. With fear-induced anxiety, we want the dog to confront the edge of his comfort zone and condition him to learn that there is no need to feel fear. However, with associative-memory anxiety, we want to build a positive association with a specific trigger. The fear-induced dog suffers a more wide-ranging fear, whereas the AMA dog's fear is only stimulated by a specific trigger. Therefore, when treating AMA, we never want the dog to feel the influence of the negative association. By giving voice to the negative association, and allowing it to be felt by the dog, our ability to construct a positive association is diminished. The ideal method is to introduce our dog to the trigger without him showing any sign of anxiety, and begin conditioning a positive association without the destructive impact of the negative association being allowed to kick in.

The ideal method

The ideal method looks like this:

1. With our trigger (ret hat man) and context (garden) set up, we introduce our dog to the same context (bring him into the garden) but don't drive him so close to the trigger as to make his anxiety warning signs appear (see the warning signs in the 'Aggression' section). The dog's introduction to the context must be well-controlled with the owner firmly in charge; the dog needs to feel the comfort and security of the owner's leadership. The owner puts the dog to 'heel', and brings plenty of treats and a favourite toy. Ideally, the dog will be able to notice/acknowledge the trigger from a distance without anxiety signs being triggered, though it is not necessary to push for this on the first few tries.

2. Once the dog is introduced to the context without showing anxiety, he needs something to do which feels enjoyable and secure. Running through a few training exercises is ideal – this keeps the dog under close control, focuses his attention on the

exercise and not on the trigger, and gives him lots of fun as he enjoys earning rewards for completing the tasks set for him. The owner can run him through a few sit/down/stay/pawshake drills. A game with the toy also works, but means the dog isn't under such secure control – there's more risk of his attention being lost to the trigger. The 'touch it' command (p240) is also a great way to focus his attention in a controlled, enjoyable way. Whether training or playing, the owner makes it really enjoyable for the dog with lots of enthusiastic encouragement, praise, and rewards. It needs to be fun, because the owner is conditioning the dog to feel good in the presence of the trigger.

3. The conditioning process above needs to be repeated so the positive association can be strengthened firmly. Over the repetitions, the dog should be able to get closer to/pay more notice to the trigger without anxiety being triggered. To help with this, the trigger can become more noticeable (if possible for the type of trigger being used). In this example, the red hat man can start to make a bit of noise or movement. If the specific trigger allows, it can get more involved – perhaps by offering treats to the dog. This should really help to build positive association.

4. After thorough repetition, the owner should vary the context. Here, we might take the red hat man out on a walk and condition the dog there. Then we can look for a more challenging context – perhaps a wooded place which is more similar to the context where the AMA is most powerfully triggered.

The conditioning – the training exercises/fun game – allows for positive association to be built. The dog will start to associate the trigger with the idea that something fun and nice is going to happen to him. If we can manage this without any anxiety being allowed to be triggered, it makes those positive associations much easier to build.

So what about the less ideal method? What if, at the first hint or whiff the dog gets of the trigger's presence, he goes into anxiety mode and it's just impossible to get him within the same time zone as the trigger without him feeling anxious?

In such cases, we might re-examine our choice of starting context. Is there somewhere else we can try where the dog might feel more at ease, or where his attention might not be so focused on the trigger? Or we could make other adjustments to the context. If the dog has a good canine companion, for example, having him around might be beneficial. Anything which helps put the dog at ease. Otherwise, we must push forth with the conditioning and make it really effective so his anxiety can be put to rest as soon as possible.

OTHER EXAMPLES

Let's look at some dogs who have different types of AMA.

Max

Max managed to escape from his owner's garden, ran across the road and got hit by a car. He recovered physically from the ordeal, but not emotionally, and now gets very frightened whenever he is near a moving car.

Do we need to overcome Max's AMA? There are several things to consider. On one hand, it can be quite good for a dog to be a bit fearful of moving vehicles – his fear might prevent Max from getting wrapped around another car bumper. On the other hand, Max lives in a town and has no choice but to be (safely) near moving vehicles when he leaves the house with his owner. If he lived in a more rural location, it might not be necessary to overcome his AMA, but he frequently encounters vehicles and the AMA is causing him a lot of distress. His anxiety causes him to behave unpredictably, which makes the proximity of traffic even riskier. So in this case, we will work to overcome it.

The trigger is a moving car. There's no point conditioning Max with a stationary car, because this is something entirely different to him and we wouldn't be addressing the source of anxiety. The context for the anxiety to be triggered is a busy road where Max walks close to the traffic along a pavement. It is not just the road where he had the accident, but any similar road around town.

What would be a good context in which to start conditioning Max? We look to make it as comfortable, and safe, as possible for him. Ideally we need to find a place where he feels happy, but where the trigger of moving cars is still present. A good place might be a park where Max likes to go for walks – one which has a car park. Here, Max will have the positive association of going for a nice walk, and we can condition him a safe distance away from the cars which are gently moving in and out of the car park.

We let him enjoy his walk first, so his positivity is boosted by endorphins and his excess energy is vented. As we return to the car park and the moving cars, we start the conditioning process (as outlined above) *before* he gets so close to the car park that his negative associations are allowed to manifest. On repetition, we should be able to get closer, increasing his comfort level. Then we can change the context – a quiet road on a housing estate (though his anxiety may be heightened if this is not a place he is familiar with). Once he's conditioned here, we work on conditioning him near the type of busier road he encounters around his home.

The best conditioning to do with Max would be some 'heel' training, as this will help reinforce his inclination to remain close to his owner and safely under control when he is near traffic.

Sally

Another car themed one – Sally used to travel quite happily in the back of the car, until she had to go to the vets for an operation on her leg. Now she is horrified by the prospect of getting into the car because she associates it with the discomfort she experienced on the operating table.

Do we need to overcome this AMA? Quite an easy decision here. Not being able to travel comfortably will have a detrimental effect on Sally's life; she won't be able to go and enjoy walks apart from the ones near the house, nor will she be able to go to the vets again in peace. It should definitely be overcome.

The trigger is the family's car with its back door open. We can't help her by conditioning her with a different car, which might seem like a nice gentle step to take, because her AMA will still trigger when she gets into the family car. At first, it's hard to judge the context – is Sally's AMA only triggered when the car is parked on the driveway at home, or does it start no matter where the car is parked? We need to investigate, so we'll drive the car a short distance away from home, then walk home to collect Sally, then take Sally for a walk and finally bring her to the spot where the car is now parked. We've changed the context, and can see whether Sally's AMA is triggered. If not, then we can load her happily into the car and start conditioning (see below).

If her AMA is still triggered, then it would seem context does not have influence, so we're going to have to condition her to be happy near the car before thinking about getting her inside it. We use the conditioning method, working on getting her gradually closer to the car. We might be able to make the prospect of getting her into the car more appealing by putting her bed or crate in there along with some of her familiar toys, a few treats, and perhaps a canine (or human) friend.

If we can get Sally into the car when the context is different, then we condition her to enjoy the car ride. We'll need an additional person to help here – someone has to drive the car while the other person works on conditioning Sally. We make the car ride fun with the help of some treats and affection, and we make her association with the car more positive by showing her that the car can take her to a really great place – we drive her to a fantastic swimming place or somewhere else she will really love.

Cherry

Before her new owner adopted her from the rescue shelter, Cherry lived in a household with some children who were too rough with her. Now she gets terribly anxious around small children because she associates them with feelings of pain and discomfort.

Do we need to overcome Cherry's AMA? Yes – it is currently dangerous for her to be around children. The question of *should* we overcome her AMA, however, has a more unattractive answer. It would be very difficult to go through the conditioning method in a way that would absolutely guarantee no children were going to be hurt as a result of Cherry's anxiety. Furthermore, it is also difficult to know for sure that AMA has been entirely eradicated, so we would never get to the point where Cherry could freely interact with children.

Unfortunately, the best we can do with an AMA like this is to adjust the dog's lifestyle appropriately. We arrange things so that she does not have to be around children so that she does not have to suffer anxiety and no one's safety is in question.

.

OTHER ANXIETIES

NOISE ANXIETY

Being frightened by loud noises is a natural survival response from all animals, including dogs. It is common for dogs to be frightened by the natural sound of thunder, and even more common for them to be frightened by the unnatural sound of fireworks.

Sometimes, noise anxiety can be confused for associated-memory anxiety. I knew a dog who collided with a car on bonfire night while fireworks were going off. Although she had suffered no previous fear of fireworks, after the crash she was terrified of them. But this wasn't due to her animalistic fear response to the noise, it was because she associated that particular noise with pain. So consider whether there may be an association playing on your dog's mind when she responds to loud noises, and treat her associated-memory anxiety using the previous chapter.

Fireworks are such a common problem for dogs that you can now buy a whole host of products to help their anxiety around bonfire night or the fourth of July. Body wraps, calming sprays, and even medication are among the things that some dog owners turn to.

Here, we'll look at the training methods we can work on with our dogs, rather than the products we can buy. Training away the dog's noise anxiety is possible for a lot of dogs, but does require persistence. It's not something you can start on the third of July hoping your dog will be all ready to enjoy the next day's celebrations; instead it should really be started months in advance.

Prerequisites are a good, solid, trusting bond between dog and owner (see 'LEADERSHIP ANXIETY' for help with this) and a safe environment where your dog feels comfortable and secure. If you have recently moved home, or your dog doesn't currently seem happy with his home environment, refer to 'ENVIRONMENTAL ANXIETY' later in this chapter.

Our fundamental approach is to use a mix of conditioning and desensitisation. We condition the dog to feel comfortable with the sound that triggers his anxiety by building positive association, and desensitize by getting him gently used to the sound. For this example, I'll refer to fireworks as the trigger of noise anxiety – but the same method can be used for other sound stimuli.

Desensitisation

For this, all we need is a recording of fireworks sounds. This is easy to find on YouTube, but make sure it can be played through speakers which make it sound realistic. Tinny speakers on a tablet or mobile phone won't be any good, because when it comes to hearing real fireworks the dog will think it's an entirely different sound. Desensitisation happens while we are conditioning (see below) and starts at a volume that is low enough not to trigger any anxiety from the dog. It is easier to build a positive association from the offset, rather than trying to override anxiety triggered by too loud a volume.

Conditioning

We use a similar conditioning method to the ones used for other anxieties, such as associative-memory anxiety, but here we're going to empower the conditioning with the help of specific items which are only enjoyed by the dog when the fireworks sounds are playing. I call them the noise toys, and they can include:

○ a 'security blanket' which has the owner's (sweaty) smell all over it.

○ A particularly stimulating and exciting (but not threating) toy such as a stuffed KONG.

○ Really tasty treats.

The special thing about these toys is that the dog *only* gets them during conditioning sessions with the fireworks noises. This will allow for a specific and powerful association to be built between the sound of fireworks and really lovely things. So the delicious treats you use have to be something which your dog won't get at other times.

To further assist with the building of this powerfully positive association, we're going to use music (unless your dog hates music). It needs to be the same piece of music each time, and should also be something your dog will only hear during conditioning exercises. I use a channel on YouTube called 'Relax My Dog' (no association with the author). It has videos which just play music that is supposedly calming for dogs – there are even special videos for fireworks anxiety. Whether it actually has calming effect or not doesn't matter at all. What's important is that through conditioning and building of positive association, hearing the music will help the dog feel more positive and comfortable. Hopefully you've got an internet-connected computer – it will need to handle the music in one window, and the fireworks sounds in another.

Conditioning exercises should take place indoors, in a place where your dog feels comfortable, and in a place he'll be able to access when the fireworks start for real. Specifically for fireworks, the exercises should take place when it's dark outside to prepare for realistic conditions.

We start each conditioning session with (at low volume) the sound of fireworks played. It is important we start with this because we will want the sound to trigger positive association of the good things to follow, rather than the good things becoming a troubling sign that scary fireworks are about to be heard. Remember that the sound must be of a low enough volume not to trigger any anxiety.

If the dog gets upset by the sound, we don't console him. This risks sending him the message that something is amiss and affirms his anxiety. We stop the sound and play with him in the garden for a bit to quickly extinguish the anxiety. We try again later, with a lower volume.

With the fireworks quietly popping away, we now start the music playing.

Now for the good times. Our job is to make the dog feel just fabulous, but we don't want to overwhelm him. Have his security blanket nearby, feed some treats, let him play with his special noise toy, and do whatever you know your dog most enjoys. I always advocate some training exercises, because most dogs really enjoy accomplishing tasks and earning a reward – but training also gives them a sense of security, too. Just make sure your dog's having a blast – to the sound of blasts, and the special music.

Repeat the conditioning session every few days, and work on desensitising your dog by increasing the volume of the fireworks incrementally. Take it slowly, and do it over the course of a couple of months. With repetition, a powerful web of positive association will be built. He will associate the fireworks with the sound of the music, which has its own positive association with the really enjoyable playtime/training/treats that follow.

As we get closer to the time of year for real fireworks, we start shaping a routine around the conditioning exercise. Most crucially, this should involve a good bout of exercise before you begin conditioning. We take him out for a good walk or play session. He'll get tanked up on endorphins and won't have any excess energy that might otherwise be spent on anxiety.

When the season rolls around for real fireworks to be heard, I recommend precisely recreating your conditioning sessions – this means playing the firework sound on your computer along with the music and fun activities. We remember to check our own composure. If we suddenly get all tensed and nervous because we're worried about our dog's response to real fireworks, he's going to suss that something's up.

This conditioning/desensitisation method might seem like a lot of work. But we should bear in mind that the dog's enjoying every moment of it, it strengthens the dog/owner relationship, and it beats pumping him with 'calming' drugs.

TRAVEL ANXIETY

Conditioning can help the reluctant traveller become more comfortable, and it begins before getting in the vehicle. Start by walking your dog around the car, in a 'heel' so he feels secure under your leadership, giving treats generously. If he sniffs at the car, praise his non-anxious interest in it. If he's getting stressed, work on conditioning him at a distance. When he's comfortable being close to the car, put some treats on the bumper or on a seat where he can reach in and take it (without having to get in). Repeat a few times, then try with the engine running. Keep him happy, and keep leading him so he feels comfortable and secure. Reinforce his positive association with the vehicle, and then we can progress to getting him inside it.

One thing to consider for the anxious traveller is a crate. Having your dog ride in a crate while you're on a car journey could help him feel more secure – but only if he's used to one. See the 'TRAINING' section at the end of the book for help with crate training your dog.

The best way to get your dog into the car will depend on your dog's individual character, but it should be left up to him to take the leap. Don't force him in, as this will only exacerbate the anxiety. Here's some approaches you can try:

Lounge about in the car as if you're just relaxing on your sofa. Don't look at your dog, just put on a show of having a nice, relaxing time. This might encourage him to rethink his perception of the car as being a frightening, growling monster that whisks him off to the vet. Now that the car just looks like a nice piece of furniture, he might be tempted to join you. If he does, just relax with him inside it. Give a couple of treats. Don't suddenly shut the doors and drive off! Get out of the car, and repeat the exercise later.

Other dogs might prefer to see the car as a place for a game rather than as a piece of relaxing furniture. Run around the car and see if your dog will chase you. Open the doors, hop in one side and out the other; if you're being fun enough, your dog might follow you through. Repeat a few times, then start pausing on the seat – just for a moment – so your dog is with you in the car. On subsequent repetitions, increase the length of this pause, and feed a few treats while your dog's with you in the car. Work on increasing the length of the pause until he can sit comfortably.

Use treats to encourage your dog into the car. Encourage him near it with a treat. Encourage him to poke his head into it by putting a treat on the outer edge of the seat. Then put a treat a bit further in. If your dog's clicker trained, click before he takes each treat to reward each step of his adventure into the car.

Once your dog's in the car, don't rush too quickly. Just spend some nice time in there with him, doors open, engine off. Talk to him, give him affection and some treats. Show him it's nice to be in the car. Having some toys and security blanket might help him enjoy it.

Take as long as you can to repeat this, several days at the least. Then start doing it with the engine running. Then, finally, start shutting the doors when he gets inside.

The first couple of journeys should be really short – a couple of feet. Keep offering treats and making it nice for him, so he gets happy with the movement of the car. Gradually lengthen the journeys, and reward him for staying clam with treats. When you think he's ready for a longer journey, take him to a really great (but nearby) place where he will have a wonderful time – and drive gently!

ENVIRONMENTAL ANXIETY

In this section we'll look at two forms of environmental anxiety: firstly, the dog who displays anxiety in the home environment, and secondly the dog who gets anxious in contexts unusual to him.

1. In the home

Environmental anxiety can often be a factor in dogs who have been moved to a new home, and can manifest as destructive or aggressive behaviour, restlessness, barking, escape attempts, and defecation/urination indoors. Not the sort of things for a good housewarming party.

The onset of environmental anxiety can be prevented by avoiding a few mistakes which some owners innocently make, especially when moving house. These include:

- allowing the dog too much initial freedom when first introducing him to the new home.

- Not allowing the dog enough freedom (contradiction clarified below!).

- Not being clear enough with rules and boundaries from the offset.

- Using punishment rather than positive reinforcement for infractions such as carpet-weeing.

- Introducing the dog to the home at the wrong time.

A good introduction, which avoids these mistakes should go like this:

We make sure the time for introduction is right: the house is ready; it's not full of unpacked boxes or removal staff trooping in and out. The environment needs to be settled.

Before bringing the dog into the home, we take him for a walk through the surroundings. This allows him to investigate the new sights and smells, and gives him a sense of place. It helps him to understand the change of locations, preventing confusion and dislocation which can contribute to anxiety.

Then we bring him home, making sure that we have dog-proofed it first. We don't allow him to just roam freely through his new house. Although we might think he'll have fun exploring it, he is more likely to feel secure and comfortable if he is guided through it under our leadership. So we walk him through the house, on the lead, one room at a time. We start with the outside of the house, praising and treating thoroughly if he goes to the loo in the garden. This might not happen, as he's just been on a walk, but it's worth being patient for the possibility. Then we go to the room where his food and water will be – making sure there is food and water already in place. We take our time, allowing for sniffs around each room, not rushing to the next. We praise his calm interest in his new environment. If there are rooms where the dog will not be allowed to go, we make sure the doors have been closed beforehand and we don't take him into those rooms. We mustn't be too flamboyant a tour guide, even if we're excited for him to see his new home – we keep things calm and positive, always praising and rewarding his calm interest.

The next step is to find the dog's 'den' – this is the spot where he will immediately feel most secure, and will likely turn into his preferred napping place/retreat in the long term. At this point, we need to allow a bit more freedom. If there are any rooms where we don't want our dog to establish his 'den', we close those doors. Then we let him off the lead, and allow him to settle. His exertion from the earlier walk will encourage him to find a resting place, and he'll chose the spot where he feels most comfortable.

It's vital that he be the one who finds this place. An owner who (even unwittingly) forces the dog into a 'den' where the dog is not at ease will cause the dog to feel anxious in this new environment. We let the dog settle down; he might need to be left alone for a bit to do so. Then we place his bed, crate, familiar toys, etc. in the spot he has chosen.

Of course, if the move has already occurred, then it's too late to conduct it in this way. But these things can still help in a retrospective fashion. Take your dog on controlled, on-lead tours of the house, so he can come to terms with the place while feeling secure under your leadership and your praise of his calm interest. Reassess the location of his 'den', especially if he seems to favour a different spot. He may feel more at ease if he is able to see his surroundings, so see if you can allow him a view through the windows. His wolf ancestors tended to sleep in open spots where they could see all around. This could make him more at ease, even if you have to put a ramp or steps in place.

You can help condition him to feel secure and happy in the home by doing plenty of training exercises. Keep practising 'heel' with frequent on-lead walks through the house; use his trust in your leadership to strengthen his confidence.

Toilet trouble

Dogs are naturally inclined not to wee or poo near in living/sleeping space, so if your dog is going to the loo indoors, it suggests he is not yet feeling secure in the environment. It doesn't yet feel like 'home' to him. If he only does it in a couple of rooms, it may be that he's just not used to those rooms yet. If he's doing it anywhere, then he's not yet at ease with the whole environment. Let's consider how to address this.

First, you can condition him to only relieve himself outside. It helps if he has open access to the garden via an always-open door or dogflap; otherwise, you need to anticipate and be alert to the times when he needs to go. Positive reinforcement will see the most benefit here, so praise and reward as soon as he goes to the loo outside. It might help to take him on frequent walks through the garden initially, rather than leaving it up to him to go outside when necessary.

A good tip for encouraging male dogs to wee outside: have a male human wee where you want your dog to wee. The smell will encourage the dog to go in the same place. Praise and reward when he does so. This will be really interesting for your new neighbours.

Punishing him for toileting indoors will not do any good; he won't understand what he's done wrong and if it happened some time ago, he won't remember. If you catch him about to wee on the carpet, distract him without scaring him. Call his name or clap your hands, then take him outside and praise/reward his wee in the garden.

Conditioning in this way can be effective, but it still leaves his underlying unease with the home environment that prevents him from seeing it as his living/sleeping space. Therefore, you need to keep conditioning him to feel secure in it, as described above. Spend plenty of time with him, working on your training exercises and playing throughout the house. Exercise him in the garden so he sleeps easily indoors; he'll lose inclination to wee around the places he sleeps.

More trouble

Let's listen to some real-life situations of environmental anxiety in the home:

I recently moved to my mum's house with my two-year-old Pomeranian. She's never known any other home apart from our old one. She has homesickness and is getting more and more frightened of me. I tapped her on the nose yesterday for going to the toilet in the house. She yelped then ran under my bed. I set up the bathroom as a place where she can go and calm down, but she goes crazy! She barks and claws the door down!

A distressing element here is the dog's increasing fear of the owner. We'll immediately spot one cause of this – the physical punishment for weeing indoors. This fear is compounded by her environmental anxiety. Severe anxiety can cause dogs to fear their owners, and even to show aggressive behaviour toward them. The owner has also made the mistake of forcing the dog into a 'den' which the dog has not chosen herself. The owner believes the dog's behaviour is due to homesickness, and does not realise the actual cause is unease in the new surroundings. The owner needs to work on positively conditioning the Pomeranian to help her feel secure in the new house. A stronger bond between dog and owner also needs to be developed by working on leadership anxiety.

Our Shih Tzu has recently become afraid to go into the garden. He is quite happy walking around the neighbourhood and has some good dog friends. We don't understand why he's suddenly frightened of the garden. We moved to this house earlier in the year and he used to be absolutely fine with going outside. He is perfectly happy being inside.

It would be nice to know exactly what's going on in this little chap's head. It would seem that he adjusted well to the move and doesn't have anxiety in the house or in the wider surroundings, but for whatever reason he has become frightened of the garden. There is a variety of possible factors in play. Something in the garden, or a noise audible in the garden, could be triggering associative-memory anxiety. Perhaps he was stung by a bee, or otherwise hurt, while out in the garden and he now associates it with pain. We can't be sure. But he is clearly suffering some form of fear-induced anxiety triggered by the garden, so the owner must work on rebuilding the dog's comfort using the methods outlined in the 'fear-induced anxiety' section.

In our new house we have an open fire, and our dog is terrified of it. She has never experienced it before because we had an electric fire in our old house. At first, she ran from the room whenever the fire cracked and popped. Now she runs away when she notices I am about to light the fire. I don't want her to be frightened, but I need to stay warm!

New objects can often cause triggered anxiety in dogs. See the next section in this chapter for how to deal with this.

2. In the wider environment

Bernie, a three-year-old cocker spaniel, is pretty typical of the sort of dog who experiences anxiety in environments away from home. He's perfectly happy at home, but had a rather safe and sheltered puppyhood which did not expose him to new experiences and places at an early age. Like all dogs, Bernie is a creature of habit and routine. His sheltered puppyhood never got him into the habit of going beyond the familiar boundaries of his home, so he now gets really anxious when his owner takes him out.

On walks, Bernie's anxiety clearly manifests in his tense body, his clinginess to his owner, and his readiness to show aggression.

What we really need is for Bernie's owner to take him back in time to when he was 10-14 weeks old. This stage marks a psychological window in the puppy's development, where new experiences are imprinted on his mind. It's a key stage for socialisation and for experience of new places – if the puppy gets used to these things at that age, it really helps his chances of taking well to new experiences, places, people, animals, etc., later in life.

Sadly, Bernie's owner isn't a time-travelling Doctor Who, but is committed to helping Bernie live a more wide-ranging and enriching life. She will start with the following principles:

1. She plans Bernie's first 'outing' by choosing the location wisely. It should be a new place but one which Bernie won't find too threatening, and one where people's safety is not going to be jeopardised if his anxiety manifests as aggression.

2. She gets him used to wearing a muzzle (see the training section at the end of the book).

3. She starts moulding her own behaviour around Bernie, adopting a constantly confident and calm composure. When he shows anxiety on his outing, it is important that she, the owner, doesn't affirm his anxiety by consoling or comforting him.

4. She works on firming up a training routine with Bernie, and practises running through 3-4 different exercises which include 'heel'. This routine is what will keep Bernie occupied and his attention focused on the outing. If and when he shows anxiety, rather than comforting him, she will refocus his attention by running through one of her chosen training drills.

And here's what happens when she and Bernie are ready for their first prepared outing:

1. The owner builds positive association before leaving the house. She has Bernie sit to put his collar (and muzzle) on, and gives him a treat for his calm obedience. This feels good for him, because he is immediately secure under her leadership and enjoys the reward. It sets the mood which needs to be maintained for the rest of the outing.

2. Bernie has always been happy driving in the car, so his owner takes him to a new park where he hasn't been before. If he were an anxious traveller, she would have to find somewhere reachable by walking from home and address his travel anxiety as a separate issue at another time.

3. When arriving at the park, she opens the door of the car and attaches the lead to Bernie, but gives him time to sniff out the new surroundings. However, she doesn't let him dictate the pace; it is important (for Bernie's own sense of security) that she remain in control of proceedings. So after a few moments, she encourages him out of the car – with a treat if necessary.

4. The walk starts with Bernie in a heel, and his owner sets a fairly quick pace. This helps him to feel that she is control, and gives him more security. She rewards him with frequent treats for his good heeling.

5. The owner is mindful that anything could trigger Bernie's anxiety, so she is constantly watching for his anxiety warning signs (see 'AGGRESSION'). She doesn't walk him along the busiest paths on this first attempt, because she knows the proximity to possible perceived threats will almost certainly trigger anxiety.

6. At one point in the walk, some joggers trot past on one of the paths. Bernie and his owner are still off the path, but he notices the joggers. His eyes fix on them, his ears become tense and his tail stiffens. Uh oh! Fortunately, the owner's attentiveness to the warning signs allow her to act promptly.

7. The owner doesn't change her composure – she doesn't try to comfort Bernie. She maintains calm control. She doesn't back

away and take Bernie away from the joggers, as this would affirm his feelings of anxiety. It would send him the message that yes, something is wrong, and we need to get out of here. Instead, she focuses his attention on something positive – she presents a treat (perhaps an extra special one reserved for crucial moments) and asks him to sit for it. They've been working on their training at home, so Bernie is able to comply and earns his treat. If the joggers have gone, the owner will get him back into heel and proceed. If they are still close, she will have him perform a down, another sit, etc. to buy some time, or just get him in a very close heel with a treat in front of his nose.

8. Later in the walk, the owner spots a cyclist who Bernie hasn't seen. She focuses his attention using the 'touch it' exercise (p240) to prevent anxiety being triggered.

9. The owner keeps the outing pretty short, because she is aware that Bernie is under some duress (though her good leadership has minimised this) and because she wants the outing to have the best chance of being successful. He'll need more exercise, so she'll take him to a more familiar place later where he can burst around safely. She takes him back to the car and gives lots of praise.

The walk was well managed, and the owner was attentive to Bernie's warning signs so his anxiety was never allowed to flare up. The training and treats helped him to begin building positive association with the unfamiliar place. Bernie's owner will keep taking him back to the same park to repeat the successful outing, but will also throw new and increasingly challenging places into the mix as she senses his growing confidence.

TRIGGERED ANXIETY

This is when a dog's fear is triggered by a particular object, sound, or other specific stimulus. It differs from fear-induced anxiety, because it can appear in dogs who are generally confident until they are confronted by this specific trigger. The fear-induced anxiety dog, on the other hand, will have his fear triggered by a range of stimuli. Noise anxiety is also different to triggered anxiety, because noise anxiety is a rational and natural response to a loud, sudden stimulus whereas triggered anxiety can often seem irrational. There is no association with pain or trauma in the dog's past, there is no potential danger posed by the stimulus, it is just something that happens to frighten the dog.

Examples of things which can stimulate triggered anxiety include:

o   shadows

o   household objects, kitchen utensils, etc.

o   snow

o   the dog's own bed, food bowl, water bowl, etc.

o   watering cans

o   joggers

o   curtains

o   dog toys

o   saucepans

- o leaves

- o feather dusters

- o bubbles

….and so on. Absolutely anything can set off triggered anxiety. Sometimes there is a blur in the distinction between triggered anxiety and noise anxiety. If a dog is frightened of lawnmowers or vacuum cleaners, this could be either form of anxiety and it does not really matter which method is used to treat it. If one method proves ineffective, the owner can try the other.

A lot of dogs can live quite happily without needing to overcome their triggered anxiety if it does not interfere with their daily routines. If a dog suffers triggered anxiety stimulated by clowns, for example, the owner can just avoid taking him to the circus.

But sometimes a triggered anxiety will crop up which can make things awkward – a fear of his own food bowl, or of frequently used household objects such as a vacuum cleaner. We'll use the latter as an example for how to overcome triggered anxiety.

I like to treat triggered anxiety in a similar way to associative-memory anxiety – by breaking down the anxiety into the separate elements of trigger object and context. With the vacuum cleaner, the trigger is the machine when it's switched on (for some dogs, anxiety might be triggered even when the machine isn't on). The context is any room in the household.

As with AMA, when working to overcome it the trigger object has to be kept constant (always the same vacuum cleaner, always switched on), but we vary the context to make it initially less threatening for the dog. Our dog's anxiety triggers when the machine is indoors (probably because his owner has never tried to hoover the garden) so we vary the context by taking the machine outside and switching it on. When we set up the trigger and context like this, we do so without our dog around.

With the setup ready, we introduce our dog in a calm, controlled way, and condition him to be in the presence of the trigger object in its new context. So we walk our dog out into the garden in a 'heel', keeping him under control and rewarding his calm obedience with generous praise and treats. We want to avoid any anxiety being triggered, so we take things really gently at first by not pushing him to go too close to the trigger object. It's great if he can acknowledge it from a distance without becoming anxious, but on the first few attempts it will probably be necessary to keep well away from the trigger and distract his attention from it. So we keep walking him in a 'heel', run through a couple of other training drills he can easily accomplish, and perhaps have a quick game with a favourite toy – provided this doesn't compromise our control over him. We keep his attention focused on us and on the training activity, and keep it really enjoyable for him by rewarding his obedience generously and enthusiastically.

We repeat the exercise the next day, and aim to move a bit closer to the trigger object. This gradual conditioning encourages him to associate the trigger object with having a great time. Eventually, we'll be able to walk him close to the trigger and he'll be able to acknowledge it calmly. We praise and reward his calm interest when he looks at it or sniffs at it. Placing some treats on the object itself might help to provoke his calm interest in it, but we only try this when he's comfortable being close to it.

Then we alter the context to one more challenging and more like the typical context – so we place the switched-on vacuum cleaner indoors. Conditioning will now be more straightforward due to the previous conditioning in a more accessible context.

So think about how you can reshape the context for your dog's own particular trigger object. A food bowl can be taken outside, perhaps even on a walk, and filled with toys for initial conditioning. A few leaves could be brought inside. If you really want to take your dog to the circus, invite a clown over for tea.

GROOMING/TOUCH ANXIETY

Some dogs don't like to be touched. This could be due to unpleasantness endured in a previous home – abusive touch or a simple lack of touch which has alienated the dog from affection. Some dogs just don't like to have a particular part of themselves touched – especially their paws. While the paw pads are very thick and able to withstand the rigours of rough ground, the upper side of the paws are really sensitive (which helps alert the dog to potential sources of injury). This is something worth working on, as we need to inspect our dogs' paws and trim claws without causing distress.

Whatever your dog's story, we can certainly help him to become more comfortable with, and to enjoy, the human touch. The way we tackle whole-body aversion is a bit different to how we help the dog who doesn't like a specific part of himself being touched. Let's look at the latter first, using the paw as an example.

Touching paws

Tulip's got sensitive paws and gets skittish when her owner tries to touch them, because they are so sensitive. She doesn't get aggressive, but takes the first opportunity to leap away and flee to the garden. If she did show aggression, the owner would need to muzzle her when helping her to overcome this touch aversion, and take things especially slowly.

For now, the owner is going to forget about trying to get claw trimmers near Tulip's paws. She's going to need several sessions of getting used to having human hands touch them, and progress will be diminished if the added stress of claw trimmers is thrust upon her too soon. Adding a bit of time on paved surfaces during her walk will help keep claw length under control for now.

If your dog has a different part of the body she doesn't like to have touched, just replace 'paws' with that part in the following methods.

There's a couple of methods Tulip's owner can use to condition her paw touch. It's not necessary to stick to just one; we can mix it up. They should be done after Tulip has had exercise so she's not all pent up, and when she is relaxed, at ease, in her comfortable spot at home.

1. Treat distraction: with Tulip splayed out on the floor at rest, we approach her with some treats. With one hand, we touch part of her body we know is safe – the shoulder is good – and with the other we feed a treat. We keep soothingly stroking her on the shoulder, talk to her in nice soothing tones, and offer treats. Gradually, slowly, we move the stroking hand a bit further down her leg, toward the sensitive zone of her paws. Keep the tone of voice the same, keep offering regular treats. When our stroking hand reaches her limit – as soon as she shows the slightest sign of being uncomfortable, we stop moving it down but keep stroking the same spot for a moment, offer a couple more treats, and use our voice to keep her at ease, then the exercise is over. We repeat it next day and see if we can get closer to her paws before crossing Tulip's limit. Eventually we'll be able to touch her paws, then we can work on holding them for longer periods. Then, finally, when she's had plenty of conditioning and feels really confident having her

paws touched, we can bring on the claw trimmers. If Tulip is too physically active for this method to work, she might need more exercise beforehand, we might need to wait until she feels more relaxed, or we could train her with the 'settle' command (see 'TRAINING').

2. Treat on the feet: this method could help Tulip to think of a hand being near her feet as a good thing. When she's sitting or laying comfortably, we're going to sit with her, stroke her on a safe spot, and talk soothingly about what a lovely day it's been. As she's happily listening to us ramble on, we're going to pop a treat onto her paw – a quick but not startling action, without the hand touching or lingering near the paw at first. Dropping the treat just next to the paw might be more comfortable for your dog. She'll look down and find the treat. We repeat, soon allowing her to watch our hand approach (but not yet touch) her paw. If she seems comfortable with this, we can allow our hand to gently touch her paw when it leaves the treat, and linger a bit before leaving. We take it slowly and build longer touches.

3. Pawshake: this might not work with all dogs, but some will be game. It can be the least stressful method, as the dog has more agency over touch. We train Tulip to shake paws with us – a human/dog hand/paw shake. A handshake between person and beast. Rather than trying to touch her paw with our hand, we encourage her to take control and touch our hand with her paw. We can do this by putting a treat, or perhaps a toy, in our fist and showing it to Tulip. She will get the scent of the treat and probably nuzzle our fist with her nose. But this doesn't get her anywhere, as we keep our fist closed around the treat. We wait until she gives up using her nose, and tries to 'bat' the treat

free with her paw. Immediately, as soon as the paw makes contact, we praise Tulip and let her have the treat. If using a clicker, we click when the paw touches and then give the praise/treat. Then repeat. With practice, she'll start to learn that touching our hand with her paw gets her the treat. When her understanding of this is strong, and she's touching paw to hand quickly when we offer our fist, then we can switch to offering an open hand and work on lengthening contact before giving the praise and treat.

Whole-body aversion

Digger is an eight-year-old rescue dog. We don't know much about his history, but he shies away from his new owner's touch. The owner can get close to him; it's just when a hand is extended that Digger gets uncomfortable. He does not want to be touched on any part of his body. This is whole-body aversion.

When overcoming whole-body aversion, choosing a suitable place to practise can be important. Because Digger's new owner has made several attempts to touch Digger indoors, the dog is quick to get uncomfortable on repeated attempts. So it is best to change the context and practise outside in the garden (provided Digger feels happy and secure there). If Digger suffered physical abuse from a previous owner, this may well have occurred indoors. Moving outside helps to break free from the negative associations Digger has between the indoor environment and physical contact. And it gives both dog and new owner a feeling of starting afresh after things seemed just to be getting progressively worse in the old indoor context.

The owner is going to let Digger have a good degree of agency. Digger will make the decisions; the owner won't force contact upon him. To help Digger feel unthreatened, the owner gets into a low position on the ground – sitting or relaxing on his back. Because this is quite an unusual combination of position and context (reclining on the grass) for Digger to see the owner adopting, Digger is encouraged to come a bit closer in order to investigate.

The owner uses a similar tactic to the 'pawshake' method above. He loosely closes his fist around a smelly, high-quality treat and lets his fist sit on the floor at his side. He does not look at Digger throughout the exercise. Instead, the owner watches the sunset, or gazes at the trees above, or reads a book – anything that helps Digger feel he is not under the spotlight of his owner's attention. This will make it easier for Digger to approach the smelly fist and investigate.

If, and it might take some time, Digger makes contact with the fist – even if it's just a slight touch of his nose, the owner gently opens his fist and lets Digger have the treat. No praise needed; it's best to keep it really quiet and calm. The exercise can be repeated immediately if Digger seems comfortable.

After a good number of repetitions over a few days, the owner can start hesitating before opening his fist, waiting for a firmer touch from Digger before releasing the treat. Then more definite and lingering contact can be established. At this point, I would start making eye contact with Digger, and uttering a few quiet words of encouragement as he approaches the fist. I start moving the fist slowly, so it comes moves around Digger's head, and later his neck and back, before releasing the treat. Eventually good contact can be built up around the body.

Failure of this method is unusual if the conditions are right. These conditions include: the correct context – a place where Digger feels comfortable; a treat which is high enough in quality and smell to lure Digger's interest; a good trusting bond between dog and owner. Digger's owner might need to work on the 'LEADERSHIP ANXIETY' section before seeing great success with overcoming whole-body aversion.

.

Owners in Crisis

Let's hear from a few owners who are desperate for help with their unhappy dogs. The following are all based on real-life cases. With each one, we'll discuss possible ways we might help the dog in question.

Washington

We are getting really upset about our border terrier, Washington. We recused him from the animal shelter three months ago; he had been in the shelter for a year and a half. He is two-to-three years old. We're having several problems with him. When he knows he is going to be left alone while we go to work (for a maximum of three-and-a-half hours only), he will freeze on the way home from our morning walk. Sometimes, he just stops dead in the middle of the road. I'm sure this is due to anxiety, because he knows he is going to be left alone when he gets back home, but no amount of reassurance we give him has helped so far. Once we get him home, he won't let us leave. He runs to the doors and blocks us from going through them. It can be really awkward when we need to get back to work after lunch.

My partner was out last night and I wanted to get an early night's sleep. I decided to let Washington sleep with me in the bedroom because I knew he would be anxious if left alone downstairs. But his behaviour became extremely unusual and frightening. He kept barking at me as if I were an intruder in the room, and he was baring his teeth and growling. I was extremely distressed and disappointed, as I thought we were making good progress with Washington's training. We do not want to send him back to the shelter, but I am starting to feel unsafe around Washington.

The first few months at home can be a really trying time for a rescue dog and its owner. There's a lot going on in poor little Washington's head, but, fortunately, he's got compassionate new owners who want to do their best for him. Washington clearly doesn't like being left alone, even if it's just for a couple of hours at a time. But his separation anxiety is not so great an issue as his leadership anxiety. Blocking the doors, refusing to move during the walk, and showing aggression toward his owners are all signs that Washington does not yet feel a secure sense of place in the relationship dynamics of his new family. He has not yet identified his new owners as his leaders/parents. This means he is adopting that position himself; he is taking ownership over the doors, and attempts to show dominance over his owner at night.

His new owners have been training Washington, and they must persevere with this in order to help establish a healthier relationship dynamic. Along with this, they should follow the advice in the 'LEADERSHIP ANXIETY' section. Although the owner felt having Washington in the bedroom would alleviate his anxiety, this move disrupts his sense of steady routine – something which needs to be really stable for a new rescue dog. The owners have been giving Washington lots of 'reassurance' when he shows anxiety, but he probably receives their change in behaviour as a validation that there is something to be anxious about. They should avoid becoming suddenly reassuring when his anxiety rears its head, and focus on maintaining their calm, controlled demeanour.

It seems possible, too, that Washington doesn't feel secure in his new environment. It doesn't sound as if he has got a place in the house where he feels secure – a 'den' – so the owners might want to help with his possible 'ENVIRONMENTAL ANXIETY'.

Working on his leadership anxiety is the first step, then they can use the 'SEPARATION ANXIETY' to help make his distress with being left alone (which should itself be alleviated when progress is made with his leadership anxiety).

Zenna

Our border collie, Zenna, joined us when she was two months old; she's now six months. During most of the day she is well behaved and normal. She definitely gets enough exercise; I take her for a walk of a couple of miles every morning, and then run with her for hours in the afternoons. But something happens at about six to seven o'clock every evening. She turns into a monster. She becomes wild and vicious, and I don't think it's just playing. Her teeth come out, there's lots of growling, and she runs at me. She jumps on me and bites me, quite hard, and does this again and again no matter what I do. It's like she's possessed – there's even the wild look in her eyes to match.

It's gotten so bad that I have had to start putting her in the crate to try and get her to sleep. I trained her the same way I trained my other dogs – by ignoring her bad behaviour such as when she jumps up. But this just seems to make her all the more desperate for a reaction. Again, this is not normal puppy behaviour. In the evening she ignores all her toys and treats and just tries to attack me.

Ah, the dreaded six o'clock 'happy hour'. Despite the owner's belief that this is not normal puppy behaviour, in a way it is. That time of the evening is the classic time for young dogs to become very active and often a little too playful. Obviously it goes a bit far in Zenna's case, but it seems as if normal puppy behaviour is being exacerbated into something verging on the unpleasant.

So what could be exacerbating this behaviour? The owner certainly does give plenty of exercise, but possibly too much. Two miles in the morning followed by long runs every afternoon is a lot even for an energetic breed like a border collie. It is possible that Zenna's exhaustion is causing her to lose concentration and control over her own behaviour. Furthermore, the owner has gotten into the habit of putting Zenna into a crate in order to try and settle her, but this is not really the best way to use a crate. A dog might choose to go into her crate when she feels settled, but forcibly placing her inside one doesn't magically make her settled. Instead, it will exacerbate her exhausted anxieties and make her behaviour worse – especially once she has learned to expect being forced into a crate.

Therefore, Zenna's exercise programme needs a bit of adjustment so she is not quite so exhausted in the evenings. Her evening energy should be put to constructive use with some training sessions, and then she should be helped to 'settle' (see the training section) without being forced into a confined space.

Because her play is quite rough, she should also be trained to play properly. To do this, the owner should continue to ignore her rough behaviour, and should catch the moments when her attention does turn to a toy with praise and treat rewards.

Jester

I've got a ten-month old English bulldog called Jester. We love him but are having problems. He doesn't see either myself or my partner as being in charge. He ignores everything we say and just does what he wants. We've tried everything: we've tried being nice to him, we've tried being strong with him, we've tried shutting him in his crate, but his behaviour still continues. We have to leave him while we are out at work, but some friends come to walk him during the day. He has got all sorts of toys and stuffed KONGs to keep him happy. We try and walk him twice a day but he is not happy on walks. Sometimes, he refuses to leave the house and other times he will just pull on his lead wanting to head back home. He steals everything, chews everything, jumps on the sofa and bites at my ears. I know he is just a puppy but this seems more than puppy misbehaviour.

The owner is aware of the problem – Jester doesn't see them as being in charge; a.k.a. leadership anxiety. But there might be some things exacerbating this anxiety which the owners haven't spotted.

Firstly, there is a significant lack of consistency in the owners' behaviour – they have been nice, they have been strong – the dog doesn't know what to expect from them, and this leaves him anxious toward their behaviour rather than feeling secure. So a consistently calm and compassionate composure needs to be adopted by the owners, as well as consistency with rules and routine.

Similarly to Zenna, Jester has been shut into a crate in an attempt to force him to settle. He needs to be helped to settle first.

Perhaps the friends who walk Jester have had better luck showing consistent leadership, so Jester feels more comfortable walking with them than with the owners. He possibly prefers walking with the friends. The fact that walks are proving unsuccessful means Jester has lots of pent up energy which gets vented through anxiety and destructive behaviour. It's really important to get the walks working, so the owners need to turn the walks into a positive experience. If Jester is reluctant to leave the house, then the owner can stand at the door with a favourite toy – ignore the dog until he approaches, then give praise and a treat. Work up a greater distance until he is leaving the house. Make walks a more exciting and fulfilling experience by having fun on them – have some playtime with the toy, and do some training exercises on the walk.

The steal, chewing and ear biting are, to an extent, signs of normal puppy behaviour but will be diminished if his energy has been put to more constructive use via walks and training. Jester should also be trained to play the right way, as we looked at with Zenna above. Get him out of the habit of biting by closing down all interaction when he begins doing this – so when he next nips ears, the owner should become a frozen, boring object. When Jester's attention turns to one of his toys, the owner can spring back to life, praising generously, and enjoying a game with the toy.

Penny

I have recently rescued a four-and-a-half-year-old Labrador mix called Penny. In the house she is fine but she suffers from anxiety on walks. At times she will just freeze and refuse to move any further. A couple of times she has got off the lead and just runs off. I'm really worried she might get hit by a car if this keeps happening. I adopted her because I need an emotional support dog, so it's really concerning that she shows such signs of anxiety.

Penny needs emotional support before she can offer the same support to the owner. This dog has just been rehomed, so her home and walk environments are completely new to her. The owner must work on forging a strong, trusting bond to overcome the inevitable leadership anxiety which comes with a rehomed dog. While the owner works on that, Penny should be kept securely on a lead during walks.

Fundamentally, a regular routine needs to be kept consistent so Penny feels secure with what to expect each day. This means exercise, meals, training, and play at the same times every day. The walks should be in the same place, somewhere quiet with few triggers for anxiety. The owner should begin 'heel' training on walks, and focus on positive training sessions at home. Leadership anxiety is the main thing to address, but the owner should also work on Penny's environmental anxiety to make sure she feels secure in her new home.

TRAINING

Why is training so important if you want a happy dog? So that he sits, heels, stops barking, lies down, etc. when you tell him to? No doubt his obedience is useful, but it's secondary to the main reason training is so fundamental for an unhappy dog. Training shapes the type of relationship between dog and owner that a misbehaving or unhappy dog needs to see. It shows him that the owner is the leader, and he will be rewarded for doing what the owner commands. While this sort of obsequiousness might seem repugnant to humans, it feels great for dogs. It brings them that crucial sense of comfort and security which is so conspicuously lacking in dogs who misbehave.

So even if your dog never gets beyond very simple actions such as sit and stay, if you can keep doing regular training sessions with him he, and your relationship with him, will reap enormous benefits.

THE CLICKER

There is a plethora of products available to tempt conscientious owners, wanting to help their unhappy dogs, away from their money – shock collars, pressure vests, pheromone sprays, and so on. But by far the best product for helping dog behaviour is the humble clicker. It's a simple, lightweight, plastic device housing a button which 'clicks' when pressed. Unlike other some other products, it doesn't rely on delivering a pain stimulus to correct unwanted behaviour. Instead, it helps dog and owner develop their relationship in an enjoyable and fulfilling way.

The clicker is used to let your dog know that he has done something good. For example, when you ask him to sit, and he sits, you give him a 'click'. He will immediately understand that he's done a good thing, he'll know he's about to be rewarded with a treat, and he'll be more inclined to repeat the sitting action next time you ask for it. The same goes for any other action and behaviour – such as if he wees outside rather than on the living room rug.

The clicker is much more effective than verbal praise ('good boy!') and a treat, because it gives much more immediate and constant feedback. Often there is quite a delay between the dog receiving the treat and the good action he has performed, which makes it less clear to him what he's receiving the treat for. It's hard to believe what a great difference the clicker can make, but you're sure to become a believer in its powers if you give it a go.

The first thing to do with your clicker is teach your dog what the 'click' means.

CLICKER ATTUNEMENT

Clicker attunement is the process which teaches your dog to understand that the 'click' signifies he has done a good thing, and he's about to receive a reward for it. This is a simple, enjoyable process but it's worth spending a good amount of time on it over several attunement sessions – we want your dog to have a really firm understanding of the click signal before progressing to using it in proper training exercises.

Attunement is best done when your dog is nice and relaxed, such as after a good walk. Sit with your dog and have your clicker ready with a good supply of treats. Click the clicker, and immediately give your dog a treat. Repeat. Click and treat. Your dog doesn't have to have done anything to earn it yet; we're just teaching him that 'click' means incoming treat. Click and treat. Don't say anything while you're doing this – it's best that the click signal isn't muddied by verbal praise. Stop after a dozen or so 'click and treats', then repeat the session later.

You'll soon start to notice that you're dog becomes expectant when he hears the click; this means he is starting to understand the sign. Firm up the understanding by varying the rhythm a bit – leave delays between clicks. But always ensure the treat comes immediately after each click.

After several sessions, your dog should be fully attuned and you can start using the clicker in real training exercises. So let's go on to look at ways you can train some useful commands with the clicker. To help your dog's sense of stable routine, try to do training sessions roughly at the same time each day. It's best to do them after he has had some good exercise so he won't be distracted by pent up energy. Keep them fairly short and positive – lots of energetic verbal praise, and no stinginess with the treats! We must also remember the golden rule of clicker training – the click must immediately follow the action we're rewarding with no delay, and the treat should come very soon after the click.

NAME

A good first clicker exercise is to reinforce your dog's recognition of his own name. Practising this can be helpful when you want to get his attention or distract him from a potential anxiety trigger.

At home, while your dog is relaxing, simply say his name in your usual tone of address and wait for his attention to switch to you. It might take a few moments, but don't be tempted to keep repeating his name. Just wait for his eyes to fix on you. As soon as they do, immediately click and give a treat. Keep repeating the exercise to reinforce, and try it in more challenging contexts such as out on a walk where there are more distractions.

SIT

With your dog in a standing position, hold a treat in front of his nose (not so close that he can snatch it). Get his attention on it, then move it up over his head, back toward his tail. Move it slowly, so he can keep his attention on it. If you get the movement correct, he will naturally want to move backwards to follow the treat. However, because dogs don't much like walking backwards, what he'll actually do is fall into a sit position as the treat moves back over his head. As soon as he sits, click and treat, then praise. Repeat. When he starts to perform the move more readily, add the command word 'sit' as you move the treat back over his head.

DOWN

With your dog in a sitting position, show him a treat in front of his face. With his attention on it, slowly move the treat down to the space between his front paws. He'll duck his head to follow the treat. When the treat is at ground level between his paws, move it forward, directly away from his body. His head will try to follow it but he'll find he has to get into a down position to do so. As soon as he lays down, click and treat, then praise. Repeat. Add the command word when he starts to perform the move more readily.

STAY

Have your dog in a sitting position and stand beside him. We start by rewarding his ability to just sit still beside us, so look away from him, admire the trees, hum a little tune to yourself, and after a few moments click and treat (assuming he has managed to stay still). See how long you can stretch out the gap. Some dogs won't be able to sit still for long, so work on building up this length of time.

Then you can repeat the exercise, but move away from him a little. Just a step or two. Don't look at him, wait a few moments, then step back to him. Click and treat, then praise – but only if he managed to stay still. If he got restless and moved, try again later. Work on moving further away from him before coming back with the click, treat and praise. Then you can add the command word 'stay' before you move away from him.

DOORWAYS

Now your dog can stay, you might want to train him to wait for you to go through a door before he does – a good method for helping with leadership anxiety.

Find an appropriate door to practise with – a low temptation door (e.g. not one that leads to the garden) is best at first.

Ask your dog to sit and stay an arm's length from the door. Now slowly open the door and walk through. Call your dog to you when you are on the other side.

It sounds simple, but it can take *lots* of practice before your dog is able to wait. If he moves prematurely, don't reward and don't say anything, just reset him and try again. End the session on a positive note (reward him for something easy, like a sit) even if you don't succeed.

Eventually, your dog will start to get the hang of it. I don't find a command word necessary, because the sight of a door becomes enough of a signal for the dog. But I guess you could use something like 'door' or 'after me' – just start adding it when your dog sits before the doorway.

HEEL

This is best trained while out on a familiar walk, or in your garden, with your dog on a lead. Have a treat in your hand which your dog can sniff at without snatching away. Hold it at waist level, or a bit lower for a small dog, but don't stoop down. Walk forward, and entice him to walk beside you using the treat in your hand. When he's walking nicely at your side, click and give him the treat. Keep repeating.

Now step up the challenge by having him on a looser lead and letting him get away from you. Show him the treat so he comes back to your side. When he's walking nicely at your side again, click and treat. Repeat. Now try getting him to your side when he's even further away. Start adding your command word, 'heel'. Keep using the clicker and treats to reinforce his nice walking at your side.

It's not such as distinct and recognisable action for your dog as ones like 'sit' and 'down', so be prepared to do plenty of practice.

SETTLE

'Settle' is a really good thing to train for dogs who tend to get a bit hyperactive. We're going to use the clicker to encourage him just to be nice and calm and settled, and we do it by 'catching' him in that state. So, wait until one of those rare moments when your dog is naturally calm, lazing about in his bed or in front of the fire, and go to him with your clicker and treats. Stroke him, talk to him with a soothing voice, and start clicking and treating. Make it nice and calm, gentle strokes, calm voice, clicks and treats. Start saying 'settle' before each click and treat. With enough repetition, he'll start to associate the relaxed behaviour with the command word 'settle', and should be inclined to become more relaxed even when he's not naturally feeling relaxed. Start practising in more challenging conditions, such as when he's a bit excitable.

WEARING A MUZZLE

Putting a muzzle on might seem like an unpleasant prospect, but is vital to ensure everyone's safety. We can use the clicker to make it something your dog really likes. If you've tried to put a muzzle on previously, but without success, start afresh with the clicker. Buy a new muzzle to help remove any unpleasant association with the old one.

First of all, just put the muzzle on the floor and let your dog come and investigate. Whenever he shows healthy interest in it (such as sniffing it, not grabbing it in his chops and tearing off with it) click and treat. Keep rewarding him with a click and treat, along with reassuring verbal praise, whenever he sniffs or nuzzles the muzzle. Build up the association of the muzzle with positive things. Next, try gently stroking your dog with the muzzle; keep the clicks and treats coming thick and fast. Gradually move these muzzle strokes closer to your dog's head. When you think he's ready, place it lightly over his head. Click, treat, praise. Finally, try fastening it on his head.

This should be done really gradually and gently; be prepared to take several days or weeks before you try to get the muzzle on his head. The clicker and treats help us to build a positive association with the muzzle.

TOUCH IT

This is a fantastic command for keeping your dog's attention focused away from something that might trigger his anxiety. The idea is that when you say 'touch it', he seeks out your hand and taps it with his nose, which earns him a treat. The exercise can be repeated as many times as necessary to keep your dog distracted.

When your dog is relaxed at home, approach him with a treat curled in your hand. Let him get a sniff so he knows there's a treat in there, and wait for his nose to come into contact with your hand. As soon as his nose bonks your hand, click, let him have the treat, and praise. Repeat several times. He'll start to learn how to earn the treat, and will be keen to make contact with your hand. When you see him starting to grasp this understanding, add the command word 'touch it'. Start practising in more challenging contexts, such as out on a walk with distractions around.

LEAVE IT

'Leave it' is another command which can help divert your dog's attention from something. It is different to 'give', which is used when he has something in his mouth which we want him to drop. You might, for example, use 'leave it' when walking through a field of sheep and you want your dog to stop frightening the sheep with his hungry glare.

To train it, curl your fist around a treat. Let him know the treat is there. He will start sniffing at your fist, getting dribble all over your hand, in his attempts to get at it. Just wait – don't say anything and don't move your fist. Eventually, he will give up. Look sharply for the moment when his attention naturally leaves your fist – his head backs away, or his eyes look elsewhere. At this moment click immediately and give him a treat. Crucially, this must not be the treat in your fist. If you let him have that, it sends the message that he can have the thing his attention was on if he just waits. So give him a treat from your other hand.

Keep repeating, and you'll soon notice your dog diverts his attention from your fist more readily. Now you can add the command word 'leave it' when he starts nuzzling at your treated fist. Once he's got a good grasp of the exercise, practise when his attention is on other things.

GIVE

Handy for when your missing sock ends up in your dog's mouth, etc., 'give' is trained by 'catching' the desired behaviour. We have to wait for the right situation – be ready with your clicker and treat for when your dog has something in his mouth he shouldn't have. Now, wait some more – be ready to click, treat and praise as soon as he chooses to drop the ill-begotten item. Repeat by waiting for the same situation to arise again. Don't be tempted to click and treat if he drops a toy, or something he's allowed to have in his mouth, as we don't want him to feel bad about carrying a toy around.

When he starts to drop the object readily, add the command word 'give'. It can be a protracted action to train, because we have to keep waiting to catch the right situation.

CRATE TRAINING

A crate can be a good place for a dog's den – the place where he feels comfortable and secure – especially if he is unable to locate such a place in your house under his own free will. Some dogs will like it; some dogs won't. A crate should never be used to forcefully confine a dog, and the door should always be opened (or removed).

We should always let the dog get used to a crate under his own steam, but we can use the clicker to encourage his interest and to build positive association with the crate.

When you've brought the crate home, put it in a place in your house where your dog likes to go for rest. Make it comfortable with bedding and a couple of toys. Wait for him to investigate the crate. When he sniffs it, or pokes his nose inside it, click and pop a treat just inside the crate for him to take. Keep rewarding his interest in the crate. Move the treats further inside, to encourage his deeper entry. Once he's completely inside the crate, click and treat a few times to make him feel happy in there. Don't try and make him to stay in too long or the positive association will be marred. Just repeat later.

You can further enhance the positive association with the crate by serving your dog's meals in there, or giving an enjoyable treat such as a raw meaty bone inside it (see the 'DEPRESSION' section for more on bones.

Those are just some of the many things which can be surprisingly easy to train with the aid of a clicker. For more detail on training actions such as 'sit', 'down', 'stay', and many other more advanced actions, there are various books available (including my own *'Train Your Dog to Read'*).

AFTERWORD

Having looked at a range of behavioural issues, we can start to see how canine upsets form a web, interlinking with one another. Leadership anxiety, for example, forms quite a fundamental link between different issues. Often separation-anxiety sufferers have at least some degree of leadership anxiety, as do dogs who experience fear-induced anxiety.

All the advice offered over the preceding pages could be distilled into two fundamental principles for dealing with canine unhappiness: a strong, reciprocal bond of trust and confidence between dog and owner, and a lively, regular, enjoyable training regimen. I hope, over the course of those pages, you were helped to find practical ways of developing those two fundamentals, and I wish you and your dog much enjoyment, fulfilment and success as you work together toward them.

CITATIONS

'Functional brain imaging of serotonin-2A receptors in impulsive dogs: a pilot study', Kathelijne Peremans DVM, Vlaams Diergeneeskundig Tijdschrift, 2002, 71, 340-347

'Expression Studies on Wolves: Captivity Observations', Roland Schenkel, 1947

'The Wolf: The Ecology and Behavior of an Endangered Species', Lucyan David Meech, 1981

'Alpha status, dominance, and division of labor in wolf packs', Lucyan David Mech, in 'Canadian Journal of Zoology' 77:1196-1203. 1999, Jamestown, ND: Northern Prairie Wildlife Research Center

'Socio-Ecological Implications of Individual Differences in Wolf Litters: A Developmental and Evolutionary Perspective', M.W. Fox, in 'Behaviour', 41:298-313. 1972 Department of Psychology, Washington University.

Aggression Quiz Answers

1) This is territorial aggression. The dog hears the sound of what he deems to be an intruder, and does his best to make the intruder go away by using loud and frightening volumes. Only when the intruder persists (the mail comes through the letterbox) does the dog go into attack mode.

2) This is fear-induced aggression. The dog feels threatened, and therefore frightened, by the sound of the approaching postman. His subtle early sign of aggression (licking lips) indicates his anxiety. He responds to the perceived threat with growls, but when these don't work (the threat still approaches, and mail comes through the letterbox), he attacks. Unlike the previous postman example, the dog isn't attempting to protect his territory. His anxiety is more personal, because it is his own personal safety which he feels is under threat.

3) This is more likely to be pack aggression than resource guarding. Bingo identifies himself as the pack alpha, and therefore displays dominance over his food, becoming aggressive when anyone else tries to take it from him. He needs to be reminded that his owner is the true alpha of the pack. Resource guarding differs because it's a result of the dog's anxiety that his food/treat/toy may be taken from him, whereas pack aggression is more about displaying dominance.

4) This is fear-induced aggression. At first, everything is fine – the two dogs are greeting each other, alert but with no signs of aggression. However, having his lead put on makes the owner's dog

feel constrained and insecure, which triggers his anxiety. The anxiety results in aggression. The owner's apparent lack of confidence will have been picked up by his dog and compounded the situation. An owner who was good at reading dog body language would be able to discern that the dogs' meeting was likely going to be resolved in a friendly manner – the stiff tails in the air suggest confident dogs who are allowing scent from their anal glands to pass from one another. The owner could have acted more confidently to bolster his dog's own sense of confidence and security. Of course, if the other dog hadn't been friendly, this would have been a really sticky situation.

5) This is learned aggression. We can tell from the owner's description that he (understandably) hasn't persisted with the health inspection when the dog becomes aggressive. This has taught the dog that showing aggression gets him what he wants (to stop being poked and prodded). Lots of dogs get anxious in this sort of context, when some of their most vulnerable and personal areas are being examined. If the owner can work on establishing a relationship based on his clear leadership, it will result in more trust being shown from his dog.

6) This is most likely to be a form of resource guarding. The owner's lap is the resource the dog protects from the husband, who threatens to remove it from the dog's possession when he returns home. The signs of aggression (initially low but increasing growling) could indicate fear-induced aggression, but it seems from the description that the dog is probably happy with the husband in other situations. A situation like this becomes interesting when we consider issues of pack identity. We've got one dog and two human owners – who is the alpha in all this? If it's the wife, then the dog coming to sit on her lap may be a sign of the dog's attempts to

assume an alpha position. This would also explain the aggression toward the husband – the dog considers him to be lower down on the pack hierarchy than herself, so is understandably upset when an inferior member undermines her authority. Therefore, in this instance, the resource guarding is compounded by pack aggression.

Printed in Great Britain
by Amazon